"Depression afflicts over 5% of Singaporeans in their lifetime, thus ensuring that it ranks as the most common psychiatric condition in our nation, and in the West. Dr Peter Mack, an accomplished hepatobiliary surgeon, has not only developed an interest in mental health but has also been trained in a form of psychological therapy, known as regression therapy, to help persons overcome their emotional problems. It is rare, and indeed highly commendable for a surgeon to be as psychologically minded as Dr Mack, but he is an unusually gifted and compassionate doctor, who cares not only for the physical, but the emotional aspects of the person. By giving voice to the struggles depressed subjects experience, Dr Mack is doing a great service to the cause of mental health education, by demystifying depression and hopefully reducing misconceptions and myths surrounding this common illness. I warmly recommend this book to family members, teachers, and counsellors and any others who care for the depressed."

Associate Professor Leslie Lim
Senior Consultant Psychiatrist, Singapore General Hospital
and author of *Depression: The Misunderstood Illness*

"An enlightening and easy-to-read book that has been written out of love and deep compassion for young people."

Carol Loi
Genetic Counsellor

T0307515

YOU ARE NOT ALONE

Dr Peter Mack

*Understanding the Inner Voice
of Depression in Young People*

 **Marshall Cavendish**
Editions

Published by Marshall Cavendish Editions
An imprint of Marshall Cavendish International

A member of the
Times Publishing Group

Other Marshall Cavendish Offices:
Marshall Cavendish Corporation. 99 White Plains Road, Tarrytown NY 10591-9001, USA
• Marshall Cavendish International (Thailand) Co Ltd. 253 Asoke, 12th Flr, Sukhumvit 21 Road, Klongtoey Nua, Wattana, Bangkok 10110, Thailand • Marshall Cavendish (Malaysia) Sdn Bhd, Times Subang, Lot 46, Subang Hi-Tech Industrial Park, Batu Tiga, 40000 Shah Alam, Selangor Darul Ehsan, Malaysia

Marshall Cavendish is a registered trademark of Times Publishing Limited

National Library Board, Singapore Cataloguing-in-Publication Data

Name(s): Mack, Peter.
Title: You are not alone : understanding the inner voice of depression in young people / Peter Mack.
Description: Singapore : Marshall Cavendish Editions, [2017]
Identifier(s): OCN 1001725133 | ISBN 978-981-47-7990-6 (paperback)
Subject(s): LCSH: Depression in adolescence.
Classification: DDC 616.852700835—dc23

Printed in Singapore by Markono Print Media Pte Ltd

Cover design and all illustrations by Wendy Mack. Email: wendy.mzf@gmail.com

For Olivia

Contents

The information in this book is intended to provide a helpful guide to the subjects discussed. The ideas and advice given are the author's opinions and not intended as a substitute for consultation with or treatment by a qualified mental health professional. The names and identities of the interviewees in this book have been changed to protect their confidentiality while preserving the spirit of the work. The references provided are for informational purposes only and do not constitute endorsement of any sources.

Acknowledgement

The author wishes to thank all his interviewees who have kindly agreed to contribute their stories for the purpose of this book.

Preface

This book is written primarily for parents, teachers and caregivers who wish to gain a deeper understanding of the nature of teenage anxiety and depression. Parenting an anxious child is like embarking on a journey into the unknown. No matter how much we think we already know about the problem of anxiety, we still struggle to understand what is going on in our children if they are depressed. Whenever we see them in a stressed state, and not know what might push them over the edge, many of us secretly wish to have access to a control knob we can turn to lower the level of their anxiety.

Dealing with anxious children can be exasperating especially when they place extra emotional demands on their parents. I recall an incident many years ago when I was attending a Meet-the-Parents Session in the junior college where my eldest son was studying. I was then listening to a guest psychologist who was speaking on adolescent growth and developmental health. All of a sudden, from among a crowd of 200 people in the auditorium sprung a question. "Ma'am," a voice sounded desperately. "My adolescent son has stopped talking to me recently. What should

I do?" There was a stir in the audience. Several heads turned in the direction of the lady who posed the question; the atmosphere was tense for a few moments before being gently eased by the speaker, who introduced the notion of the adolescent's need for personal space.

The incident awakened me to the degree of emotional turmoil that a depressed child could possibly cause to his parent(s). In the years that followed, several of my colleagues who had depressed children, shared with me their agony of watching their children live in the midst of hidden anxiety and a confusing world of pain. More recently, when some mothers shared with me their concern over how their distressed school-aged children were struggling with suicidal thoughts, the idea of a book that could help these parents germinated.

As parents, we all want our children to succeed. However, when we find our children intensely preoccupied with their inner struggles while hoping for adults to understand them, we feel as desperate as they do. Gradually, we realise that we need to understand them as normal individuals who are just groping around for ways to deal with their own pain and longing for their close ones to connect with and show love to them. Unfortunately, they sometimes take up our full attention as parents and yet break our hearts with their behaviour even as we are establishing a safe haven for them to heal and grow. We thus end up bewildered as to how we can make sense of their inner struggles.

While planning this book, someone alerted me to a newspaper article of an 11-year-old schoolboy who committed suicide after failing his school exams for the first time.[1] Instead of facing his parents' disappointment, he chose to end his life by jumping from the bedroom window of a HDB apartment on the 17th level. Apparently, in his first four years in primary school, his mother had been expecting him to score at least 70/100 marks per subject for his exams, failing which she would cane his palm lightly, one stroke for every mark short of 70. However, his mother would also reward him with a gift whenever he did well. Unfortunately, this strategy now turned disastrous.

On 12 May 2016, when the boy got back the results of his mid-year exam and found that he had scored only 50 for English, 53.8 for Chinese, 12 for Higher Chinese and 20.5 for Mathematics, he turned anxious. He managed the situation by telling his mother that his results were "average". In return, the mother bought him a kite as a gift. Four days later, he got his Science papers back and the score was only 57.5. Tension mounted as the school's deadline for parents' acknowledgment of results was drawing near. On 18 May, he was found lying dead at the foot of the housing block with multiple fractures. In agony, the mother exclaimed that she failed to understand why the child had chosen death as the option when her expectations were not unduly high.

I was perturbed by the story. It brought to mind the potentially serious nature of perceiving a child as a small adult and managing him by adult standards of behaviour. The stress was amplified

---

1   The story has been reported in the Straits Times at www.straitstimes.com/singapore/courts-crime/death-of-boy-11-who-fell-17-floors-after-failing-his-exams-for-the-first-time

when the little being was made to earn his love from parents who set their criteria that had to be fulfilled from their vantage point before love was meted out. The child did not understand why he had to achieve something just because his parents had the power to deliver unpleasant consequences or why he had to face shame and lose goodwill if he failed. Instead, what he was more conscious of was the fact that he had been deprived of his human dignity and goodwill each time he received punishment. After pondering over it, I decided to make *unconditional love* the starting theme of this book.

In our effort to create a nurturing environment in which children thrive, we need to understand the role of parental love in esteem building in the child. We also need to be aware of his sensitivity to failure and demoralisation in a society where the education system is overly demanding and competitive.

As I started working on the manuscript, I came to know of a depressed teenage friend. The teenager is an adopted child living in a wealthy family. Despite all the material goods that she has been bestowed with, she feels that her adopted parents have not been listening to her adequately and she does not feel loved. She chooses to believe that the root of her mental predicament lies with her being abandoned by her biological parents. As her depression deepens, she resorts to self-cutting as a way of coping.

Upon hearing this story, I have further developed the subject matter of this book under an overarching theme that focuses not just on love, but also on the *inner voice of depression* in the child and how to recognise it. After all, parents are a child's most influential role model. The way they understand things, solve problems and confront challenges will teach their child lessons. If parents are able to gain a deeper understanding of the inner workings of the child, the latter will learn to reciprocate and grow up a more empathic and resilient individual.

In our hurried pace of life, it is understandable that readers are inclined to look for quick-fix solutions laid out in an easy-to-consume book that requires minimal investment of reading time and energy. I have therefore kept this book within a reasonable length, but chosen to transcend the guide-book style to one that helps readers gain insight into the root causes of adolescent depression and how to intervene to prevent undesirable outcomes. They will understand that the process of figuring out ways to help children to manage life challenges is part of their own journey as nurturers raising children.

While the workings of the inner psyche are a complex area of knowledge, the language in this book has been intentionally kept simple and comprehensible. Wherever appropriate, I have included excerpts of my interviews with individuals who have survived their adolescent depression into adulthood and were kind enough to share their experiences and life challenges.

Chapter 1

Anxiety and Depression in Young People

ANXIETY in children is a serious matter. Many of us, as parents, tend to downplay our children's anxiety with the belief that it is part of juvenile growth and tell ourselves that feeling anxious is within the norms of childhood behaviour. We assume that over time, the child will grow out of it. In the process, we overlook the important fact that children, at their age, have yet to acquire sufficient life experience to equip themselves with the skills to handle anxiety. The lack of coping skills on their part causes distress, making them feel helpless and vulnerable and confering a feeling of hopelessness. In the absence of adult help, the feeling of desperation pushes them into despair and leads to depression. By the time children reach this stage, parents sometimes discover, to their horror, that some have been inflicting physical injury on themselves as a way to cope with their anxiety.

What is Anxiety Like?

When children get anxious, they not only get nervous. In fact, every aspect of their physical, emotional and mental functioning is affected. The symptoms can be varied, from being scared of losing control of their lives to forgetting lessons taught in school. When they feel anxious, they find themselves in a tense, unsettled state of mind, or fear, as if they are anticipating a vague and threatening event to befall.

We generally understand fear to be an emotional reaction to a danger that we can identify within our immediate environment. We usually react intensely because fear tends to be specific and has the nature of an emergency. In response to the feeling of being threatened, teenagers tend to generate an anxiety that is unpleasant, objectless and diffuse in nature.

I recall having my first childhood anxiety attack in school at the age of seven. It occurred one morning out of the blue and for no apparent reason. The mental state was one of uneasy suspense due to intense agitation accompanied by tension and unexplained dread of the school environment. A part of me felt odd, strange and wrong, as if a fever was coming on. The teacher gave permission for me to leave school and return home to rest. A subsequent thermometer reading showed a normal temperature, but the feeling of agitation and fear lasted the rest of the day. The fear appeared to have stemmed from a threat of impending danger even though the threat was not real, and I did not understand what could have triggered it.

This experience highlights the main problem in dealing with anxiety—the difficulty in determining its cause. The points of onset and triggers are seldom clear. The agitated mental state tends to be persistent and pervasive in nature. Quite often the anxious feeling lingers in the background for a long time and makes the child feel unsettled and drained. Frequently, parents would react to their child's anxiety with disbelief or suspicion or by brushing it off as part of a developmental milestone.

When a child is being overwhelmed by an anxiety attack, we need to understand that the logical part of his brain has been put on hold, while the emotional part has taken over. In such a situation, any attempt to rationalise his worry away will not be fruitful. What we can do is to give the child some tools to manage his worry.

Frequently, an anxiety attack manifests itself with physical symptoms of dizziness, sweating, lump in the throat, dry mouth, palpitations or nausea. Sometimes the symptoms are less specific such as a sinking feeling, wringing of hands or trembling of legs. These symptoms can overshadow the positive aspect of a child's life and he may feel that things are getting out of control. As such, he can be frightened, and may want the parents to know and feel exactly how he is feeling and appreciate his level of distress. This is where empathic listening helps.

At other times, the child may look normal on the outside but feel that he is screaming inside. Ignoring the situation will not help. As an emergency measure in an anxiety attack, we can help by pausing for a moment and take a few deep breaths together with our child. Deep breathing has a calming effect on the mind. Once calm, we may find it easier to figure out a way of helping the child.

To the child, there is comfort knowing that he is not alone in facing anxiety, and there are fellow sufferers who can empathise with him. It is also good to make him aware that worrying is a protective mechanism that helps him to survive danger, and that it is perfectly normal for one to worry. What he needs is a way to deal with the false alarms triggered by this protective system.

As emotions are lodged in the subconscious mind, one approach to handling anxiety is to make use of the creative potential and fantasy-loving part of the subconscious mind. The whole idea is to shape the way the child perceives his emotions. One useful technique is *personification* (to be elaborated later in this chapter). It is the art of representing the quality of the child's emotions in human form. It involves encouraging him to represent what anxiety feels like to him in the form of an artistic image or even to create a cartoon character that personifies his anxiety. Creating such a character can demystify the frightening physical response the child experiences when he worries. The process can also reactivate the logical part of his mind to regain control. With this technique, he can invite more emotion, humour, truth and human qualities into something that is non-human and allow connections to form. These connections will allow the child to see his own anxiety differently in symbolic terms and make sense of the way he is reacting to the world.

Secret Sorrows and Depression

Both anxiety and depression are common phenomena that often occur together in our lives. Modern lifestyles are characterised by efficiency, productivity and a fast tempo. We live our lives on the run, with fast food, pressing emails, rapid digital downloads and tight work deadlines. We are constantly under pressure to replace our holidays with mini-breaks. Our time is flooded with WhatsApp messages on mobile phones as we unconsciously drift into an ever-busier life that depletes our energy resources.

In this fast-paced environment, the depressed child who is too young to understand his own psychodynamics tends to feel sad and lose self-confidence. His friends find him becoming less talkative with a waning interest in life. What he used to look forward to no longer fascinates or matters to him now. He may find it difficult to get up from bed in the mornings and feel upset with trivial matters. He may feel like he is agitated or in a bad mood for no reason. He lacks concentration and cannot be bothered to do anything. A deep fatigue or laziness seems to have descended over him. He has no aversion to death and may develop suicidal thoughts with the reasoning that the family and school can always carry on without him.

As parents, we are often misled by the widespread notion that depressed children look miserable externally. The truth is that they seldom do. Depression is not always clearly and outwardly visible in the individual. A person in an anxious state often

has difficulty identifying the cause of the uneasy tension that is troubling him, and children who are anxiously struggling with stress often escape notice by the adult. Some children are capable of putting up a façade of a healthy mental state to protect their self-image. Others may experience a feeling of irritability, extreme tiredness or a difficulty in responding to other people's concern. They may turn down activities that they used to enjoy and instead opt for aloofness. Sometimes they appear tearful and cry over trivial matters.

It is a challenge to recognise anxiety and depression in young persons. Many of them have swinging moods. An integral part of anxiety is worry. A child who continually worries will be obsessed with past experiences and feel anxious about what might happen in the future. He may appear happy and confident one day and become withdrawn, silent and brooding the next day. It is seldom possible to draw a dividing line between the mood swings and depression in young people. It is not common for them to talk about themselves as being depressed, nor is it easy for them to do so. They may simply comment that they are feeling tired, bored or fed up with what they have been doing. Rarely do they recognise depression in themselves. It is important therefore, that parents, teachers and caregivers make an effort to recognise the signs of depression in children and seek help on their behalf.

Sometimes the symptoms in these young people may be very subtle. They may complain about their dissatisfaction with their outward appearance, their loneliness or their feelings of being socially unwanted after a failed romance. At other times, they may display a dislike for their schoolwork, parents or siblings. Yet, moments later, they may feel and appear normal again. By the time they develop extreme behaviours such as abnormal eating habits or self-harm, it usually means they are no longer able to manage the overwhelming emotion they have been facing. Help is clearly needed at this stage.

Traditionally, most of us perceive childhood as a period of happiness in one's life that is characterised by carefree behaviour, laughter, kite-flying, ice-cream and fun in the playground. Unfortunately, this picture has changed significantly nowadays when our children are living in a fast-paced society that is academically competitive with high demands on exam scores. With high expectations in schoolwork and co-curricular activities, busy schedules of after-school tuition classes and little time for recreation and interaction with family members, there is inevitably a gradual distancing in the parent-child relationship. This sows the seed for parental neglect. With the increasing distance, the child's emotional issues encourage the development of apathy and withdrawal.

It may be difficult to see how differently depression manifests in children and in adults. Some children do experience the classical symptoms of sadness, withdrawal, avoidance of friends, refusal to attend school, low energy level, poor appetite and concentration difficulties in their schoolwork. Others may not be able to articulate their sadness. Instead they may describe it simply as boredom or an inability to have fun. They may also sob quietly in solitude, exercise self-criticism and harbour thoughts of dying. Others may appear irritable and angry rather than sad. Sometimes they may even appear overactive, argumentative and impulsive. Underlying all these differences is the manner in which the child makes his way through his journey of adolescence.

The Adolescent's Journey

Adolescence is a period of significant physical, social and psychological change. It is during this developmental period that adolescents develop their own ideas and views. They are often intolerant of their parents and prefer the company of friends. However, depressed adolescents are usually not only intolerant, but irritable and angry at family members as well. They often have numerous anxieties that they may not want to talk about. With the trapped tension, it is hard for them to concentrate on tasks that require sustained mental effort. For this reason, their grades in school may fall. Over a prolonged period, depression and fleeting thoughts of suicide become increasingly common. Not infrequently, horrifying behaviour such as cutting of wrists or forearms may emerge as an indication of depression.

Every adolescent experiences stress at some point in this stage of his life, but many adults adopt the attitude that this represents merely a normal period of trouble and upheaval. What may not be apparent is that the stresses faced by adolescents are very variable. It is difficult to be sure which behaviour is normal and which behaviour is a result of more serious psychological disturbance. This poses a problem in that many adolescent experiences have an important and lasting impact on an individual's growth and development, particularly in the areas of self-identity, psychological stability and relationships.

Identity is that part of the adolescent's life in which he strives to express and fulfil his potential. Self-identity is not a static phenomenon. It is built on a self-concept, expressed in terms of his strivings, goals, values and expectations. This self-concept is continuously moulded by his interaction with his interpersonal environment. The self-identity eventually helps him to come up with an answer to the question of "Who am I?" in the context of a given life situation. At each stage of his development, his identity is anchored to the identity of his parents and family in a special way. The process undergoes change as he gradually gains independence from the family members.

RACHEL ON SELF-IDENTITY AND PSYCHOSOMATIC ILLNESS

Rachel is in her early twenties and had approached me for help in managing her sadness. She has one elder sister who is a family "star" while she has been scapegoated by her family members from a young age. After graduating from university, she decided not to stay together with her family members. As her childhood story unfolds, it becomes clear a lack of family love and her identity development have played significant contributory roles to her depression.

My elder sister had always excelled in school and won awards every year. My parents would joke that I was picked up from the drain, since I was living within a family of scholars. They constantly compared us: "Jie jie is the clever one and is top in every subject," they said. "Mei mei is not clever, poor in her studies but she is obedient." I grew to learn that the only consoling thought they had of me was that I was obedient. So, if I ever said or did anything that they didn't like, I felt that I would not be part of the family any more.

I struggled a lot with my identity, because in school, I was really the class clown, happy, joking and always friendly with many people. Teachers sometimes struggled with my disruptive influence as I would be chatting extensively with my friends. But at home, I was so quiet and submissive that it felt like I was a completely different person. I felt like a hypocrite. The worst thing was that I didn't even know which was the real me; it might have been neither. I only knew that I needed people to love me. In hindsight, I realised that I was willing to become whoever they wanted me to be, regardless of how upsetting the situation was, in order to acquire the love I needed.

My anxiety of not being accepted grew so obvious that even my friends found it amusing. In Primary 4, they would routinely play this game where they pretended to be angry with me, and refused to tell me the reason why. I would freak out and it drove me crazy. That's why I started cutting myself. Sometimes if I was lucky, they would tell me that they were just playing a joke on me after one week of ignoring me. Sometimes it would drag on to a month. Each time they did that, I'd cut myself.

My sister became increasingly more rebellious and started acting out when she reached Primary 6. I was in Primary 5 then. She became a school bully and started getting physical with my parents too. She would make Mum so angry that Mum would go to the kitchen and wield a chopper in our faces and threaten to chop us up. It was extremely traumatising. And after every quarrel, I remember both my sister and my mum would blame me for their fight. Mum would tell me, "See, because you walked so slowly and so I ended up quarrelling with your sister." Sis would say, "See, because you can't finish your food, I had to tell Mum not to force you. So we ended up quarrelling." I was constantly regarded as the cause of family disputes, and everyone, especially Mum and Sis, would label me as a trouble-maker.

I don't remember a period in my childhood where I actually felt happy being myself and feeling free. I never went to get my mental health checked, and the only time it was suggested that I might have an anxiety issue was when I was 20 years old and in university then. I suffered chronic chest pain that persisted for eight months straight. Sometimes it got so painful that I could not even stand up. I remember the worst episode was when I collapsed one day while crossing the road, because the pain in my chest was so bad. I went to the A&E department of the hospitals so many times, and they had all sorts of tests done. They checked my heart, lungs and organs but found nothing.

One doctor suggested that it may be a stress-related disorder, possibly anxiety, and wanted to prescribe Prozac. However, as I was studying psychology in the university then, and aware of the side-effects of this drug, I refused his prescription.

Psychological stability is the maintenance of constancy and continuity of an individual's mental state through time under the pressure of changing life circumstances. This stability assures the intactness of one's behaviour in the face of new experience. It is a function of the orientation of the self to the family. The achievement of psychological stability is influenced by the individual's capacity to cope with conflict. For the younger child, the main problems of psychological adaptation lie in the realm of child-parent and child-sibling relationships whereas for the adolescent, the main areas of concern are with sexual maturation and emotional preparation for adulthood.

Relationship issues of the growing child are closely knitted with the evolution of childhood anxiety. We are all familiar with the close attachment of the newborn infant to the mother. Typically, up to five or six years of age, the child's behaviour is governed by what he thinks will be approved or disapproved by his parents as if a moral code of conduct exists between them. Underlying this behavioural pattern is the child's wish to be loved. This becomes the driving force for him to respect his "family laws" without question and allow the parents' wishes and demands to determine his mental make-up.

As the child grows older, he begins to develop his own ideals and exercises self-judgement. He starts to have feelings of self-regard and may experience guilt and shame if he does something contrary to his expectations of himself. These expectations that originally belong to his parents now shift to become part of his own inner demands.

Psychological interferences during childhood often bring problems to adult life. Many children are troubled in themselves, but their problems remain unnoticed because they comply with outside expectations. We commonly identify the typical good and quiet boy who gives trouble to no one. All parents and teachers would like him because he does everything that he is told, obediently and without complaints. However, when we look closely at the child, we are often taken aback to discover that he has no friends and may cry secretly to himself. Worse still, he may be unable to show his distress to others because his family members expect him to be strong.

On reaching adolescence, the young person realises that his earlier childhood behaviour that has brought him parental approval is no longer useful. He now needs to seek approval and recognition from his peers instead. As such, he has to perform in a way that is acceptable to his contemporaries or else he will find that other people may not want to associate with him. Beyond the sense of isolation, he may develop sadness and the perception that he is a social failure. Going a step further, he may even start to believe that something is intrinsically wrong with him.

During the growing phase, the young person may want to choose friends whose expectations of him are such that they enhance his wish to become an adult. From the image of himself as being a mummy's boy, he wants to transform into a picture of someone who takes responsibility and ownership of his life. This is an important step towards maturation. If he is able to feel that his thoughts and feelings are his own and independent of how his parents might react, he would have taken his first positive move toward separating himself emotionally from his parents.

Unexpected psychological breakdowns in adolescence sometimes catch parents and teachers by surprise. We sometimes encounter a brilliant child who suddenly fails in school exams when he reaches adolescence. At other times, a normally behaving child suddenly commits suicide for unclear reasons. These behaviours can be dumbfounding. Deep down, the adolescent may be troubled with the perception that he is all alone by himself, failing in his achievements, not developing normally and his sorrows remain unheard.

Schools are, on the whole, a tension-filled environment. After all, it is a place that the child has to leave the safety of his home to go to. It is also the place where he will be judged and evaluated by the teachers and have to fit in with his peers or risk being bullied. Whenever our ideas about how things should be collide with how things are, emotional reactions are triggered in our mind. We torment ourselves over what has happened to our lives and the choices we make while our mind has a mysterious way of holding onto the emotional pain. When the child's emotional pain escalates to the extent that it affects his ability to function at school, then things start to be problematic.

Parents tend to regard their children as a possession and are often too focused on their responsibilities to feed and clothe them. Hence, many of us grow up in an environment where we are supposed to be seen and not heard. If a child does something outside the realms of parental acceptance, he would be steered back on course according to how the parents believe he should be behaving. With repeated conditioning from parents, the child learns to keep his thoughts to himself, and slowly loses his ability to think for himself.

Some parents behave as if they have the legal power to make all decisions for their child. The parents expect him to abide by every rule they dictate, including the choice of university education, career and friends. This is the core of an authoritarian style of parenting. They feel that they know the child better than he knows himself and that whatever decisions they make are for the child's good. Over time, the adolescent feels that his personality has become artificial and developmental growth has lost its meaning. Beneath the social mask he wears is his hidden, *shadow* side—the wounded, sad and isolated part of him, from which his inner voice of depression will later emerge.

Ruminative Thoughts

Depression goes beyond the perspective of a simple, faulty programming of the mind. In a depressed state, a person's journey into the future has halted. He feels stuck and a sense that future prospects do not exist for him. The passage of time promises a dreary repetition of the past. Without a future to anticipate or a solid self to build upon, he soon loses his vitality. It is a state of self-generated sadness, and to the person, sadness is a way of life and his outlook is always gloomy. He continuously thinks about the various aspects of situations that are upsetting and lets the problem replay over and over in his mind.

The thoughts in depression tend to run counter to rationality. They also violate the enthusiasm of life. Things just seem to be "wrong" with the individual. The depressed person has difficulty in self-expression. Carrying out a simple conversation with another person may become a struggle. He feels as if there is a glass wall dividing him from the rest of the world. The world around him appears cloudy and grey even on sunny days. He cries for no apparent reason, even at something that is insignificant. Smiling feels stiff and awkward. His senses are dulled and food tastes bland. The memory of every past failure and every bad experience comes alive. There is a torrent of negative emotions and this saps his strength. His enthusiasm is being eliminated and life is turning into misery. At his worst, he feels as if he is dead, or better off dead.

When an individual goes through a major stressful life event he tends to have a lowered ability to establish clarity of thought which in turn makes it harder for him to cope, solve problems and make decisions. Even commonplace daily situations such as time pressures, work loads or interpersonal conflicts would decrease his personal effectiveness. Under stress, the person may repetitively go over a thought or a scene in his mind, hoping to reach a new understanding of his situation and help him move on.

As the process of rumination begins, the individual will find himself facing a stream of persistent, recurring thoughts that revolve around a common theme that enters his consciousness and shifts his attention away from his task at hand. Often, rumination occurs even in situations in which nothing can be done about the problem at hand. Unfortunately, the process can be long-lasting and dominate his mental life. The occurrence of repetitive and unwanted thoughts is a potent contributor to unhappiness and further worsens the ability to solve problems.

Rumination often takes place as a reaction to sadness but the person who ruminates will tend to believe he is gaining insight through the process. Unfortunately, the repetitive thought reinforces and intensifies the feelings of inadequacy and emotional distress that he already feels. This in turn raised the anxiety level and prolongs the duration of depressive episodes, while the negative thinking continues to cripple his problem-solving ability.

Ending the rumination cycle may be difficult. As parents and caregivers, we need to first help the child to identify the fear. Guiding the child to let go of what he has no control over may help. He must identify whatever situations he can change so he can draw up a list of goals and make the appropriate changes. It can be useful to let him figure out what his worst case scenario could possibly be, and if he feels he can handle that situation then he may be convinced that there is little reason to continue brooding over his current thoughts.

Assisting the child to think of times when things had turned out fine would help to shift his attention to a positive memory network and steer him down a different path of thinking. He may want to go through pictures of happy memories and recall his joy and happiness and all the physical sensations that were associated with them. He may even want to take a walk in a location that he connects with an earlier time when things had turned out well for him and this will further help him enter into a positive frame of mind.

It is important to understand that the despair in depression is not about the person or external object that one loses. It is about oneself. If an adolescent breaks off from his girlfriend, it is not about the girlfriend that he is desperate over. It is he himself who is in despair, without the romantic partner. Likewise, if a girl loses her mother, the pain from the loss provokes her to hang on to her past memories with her mother. This suffocates her future with constraints borrowed from the past. She feels that she has lost the mother's gaze that reassures her of who she is.

I recollect an example of a college boy who had lost his best friend through suicide and was struggling with despair.[2] He described occasions when he had walked under an open sky and noticed a twinkling star. He would see it as his departed friend saying "Hi" to him from the sky. The pain of the loss made him feel that the world he lived in still carried his friend's presence.

The loss of one's job is another example of an insult from the outside world that could create a crisis and trigger depression. The loss undermines one's sense of self-worth and one's certainty about the self. Later in this chapter, Lucy, a lady in her early thirties tells the story of her depression after losing her job and how she dealt with it through contemplative meditation.

Many others may not cope so well when faced with a crisis. The person may lose track of what he wants, fears or hopes for. He may put on a show and pretend as if he knows who

---

2   The full suicide story is described in the author's previous book, *Bend Not Break: Learning from Loss*, published by Brahm Centre, Singapore, 2016.

he is because this seems to be his only alternative to giving in to the chaos of his uncertainty. The downside is that the act of pretence stupefies the person into a deceptive state. The persona that he shows the external world runs alongside a hidden self that is manipulating the showing. Unconsciously he is trying to conceal the fact that he does not really know who he is and what he wants.

Chronic illness is another example that has a huge impact on a person's life, both physically and emotionally. It is known that one in three individuals with a major medical illness has symptoms of depression. The affected individual develops a sense of not knowing what has happened to him and how much time has passed while he was struggling to recover. Fear, isolation and loss of control are commonly expressed. He may have time to reflect over his situation only when he is out of the hospital and back home. The chronic illness can cause tremendous changes to his life, making it impossible for him to do the things that he enjoys. This erodes the self-confidence and hope that he has for his future.

Although different people react to the recovery process in different ways, the majority of patients will feel emotional with the sickness at some point. Questions like "Why me?" or "What if I don't make it?" are often asked. For most people, making sense of what has happened to them is a gradual, fragmented process over a long stretch of time. A part of the individual may want to know every detail of their recovery process but another part of him may just want to forget the ordeal and move on.

CAROL ON CHRONIC ILLNESS AND DEPRESSION

Carol has been depressed over a medical condition that has been attacking her body's immune system since her teenage years. Adding to the physical stress she has to struggle with, a downturn in her emotional life came recently when her mother passed away. She shares some of the more painful experiences in her career experiences as a young adult.

At 17 years old, when other teenagers were having fun enjoying life, I had to fight a battle within me: I was diagnosed with lupus. I had to cope with the fact that I needed to take daily medication for the rest of my life and the reality of a new physical appearance that would arise from the side effects of the medication. The illness eventually took a toll on me, physically and mentally. I got really frustrated when my mother was always trying to screen me from the sun and I had to wear a cap for protection whenever I went out.

I struggled through my 'A' Levels, scoring well enough to make it to Science faculty and study my favourite subject, Botany. School days were enjoyable until graduation when I had to decide on a career path. I decided to join the landscape industry. This proved to be a challenging feat, especially when it came to job hunting. I was very honest with my job interviewers that I was sensitive to sunlight because I was suffering from lupus. The common questions I got in response were: "If you can't stay under the sun, how can you work in the landscape industry?" and "If you can't be overstressed, how can you work at all?"

I was rejected again and again in my job applications. I

was dejected until a short stint to help out at my course mate's company landed me with a full-time job. I was self-conscious and just so thankful that I finally had a full-time job. So I asked for and accepted the pay of a diploma holder instead of a degree holder. This was a decision I regretted. Eventually I became depressed over my miserable pay. My school mates were driving cars, swiping credit cards, and travelling to fancy places for their vacations while I was stuck in a contractor firm, supervising planting jobs and plucking weeds with my Bangladeshi workers whenever there was a shortage of manpower. I was stuck there for seven years with no pay increment. My friends kept nagging at me to get out of the job but they didn't understand that I was different from them.

I was overly tired and overexposed to the sun. An acute attack of lupus struck again and hit hard this time. I suffered an epileptic attack during lunch at work. When I regained consciousness later, I totally forgot what had happened. My memory function was badly affected and my world became a total blur. To this day I am very forgetful.

The Shadow Self

Treating depression requires an individual to look seriously into his unique personality and acknowledge the presence of his *shadow* self.[3]

As a psychological term, the *shadow* was first used to describe the dark aspects of one's personality, or that part of ourselves that

---

3   The term "shadow" was originally used by Carl Jung to describe those unconscious aspect of one's personality in which the ego rejects as being part of itself. The shadow tends to be largely negative and is often considered the "dark side" of oneself.

is hidden from us. It can be associated
with the unknown which is outside the
realm of conscious awareness. It can
also be associated those aspects of one's
personality that the ego does not identify
in itself. Because of our tendency to reject

this aspect of our personality, the *shadow* tends to be largely
negative and considered to be potentially harmful. The *shadow*
follows us everywhere. As long as we ignore its existence, it is
bound to affect us in ways that we do not consciously notice.

Most depressed people would claim that they are happy,
and for the most part, they appear so. However, in their private
moments, they may feel stuck with a sense of emptiness and
recall an embarrassing memory from childhood. This painful
memory then triggers a self-shaming process. This is a situation
when depression has something to say to them through their
shadow. The depression is trying to make them see those aspects
of their lives that are hurting them most, and help them realise
that they should heal these aspects of themselves instead of
ignoring them.

We are all born pure and innocent, and with a unique set
of personal qualities. As infants, we express the full breadth of
our human nature unhesitatingly, and without censorship. As
we grow up, we realise that certain aspects of our personality are
not acceptable to people around us. We are shamed for crying
and derided for wanting attention. As we mature, we learn to
repress those qualities that got ourselves hurt. It is as if we have
thrown all those undesirable qualities into a bag and buried them

within while lugging the bag on the back of our shoulder all the time. This bag is the analogy and equivalent of our *shadow*.[4] This metaphor helps to illustrate and explain how we develop a personal shadow throughout childhood and early adulthood. We learn from friends, family and our society what behaviour or parts of our personality that are not acceptable, wanted or desired and we put them into the bag.

When the dark side of our self is stuffed deeply within this bag, it is hidden from ourselves and others. The messages we derive from the things hidden in this bag are quite simple—that there is something wrong with us as the person carrying the bag and that we are not deserving and lovable enough. We tend to believe these messages and that if we look closely at what is inside the bag, we will find something horrible about ourselves. Hence we rather not open the bag.

At this stage when we are in denial of our *shadow*, we tend to project our own negative qualities onto other people. We express hostility outward onto others whom we perceive to carry the shadow qualities that we consciously fear. What is denied within us is projected outwards and attacked in others, and we remain oblivious of our behaviour. When the time comes that we are willing and able to perceive something that, until now we have hidden from ourselves, we start to confront our shadow. It is at this point that self-enlightenment occurs. Sometimes the meeting with our shadow occurs in a single moment of illumination, when connections automatically collide and reach

---

4   The analogy of the shadow self with the bag that we drag behind us has been described by Robert Bly in his book, A Little Book on the Human Shadow. Harper, 1988.

the threshold of consciousness.

Bringing together the ego and the personal *shadow* begins with facing those aspects of ourselves which have been denied. The confrontation comes from the ego which is being transformed. The desired outcome is one in which the "I" has been redefined to incorporate some newly recognised aspects of the *shadow* into the ego in a newly synthesised whole. It is like moving the battleground to the negotiating table, and is a useful way to move our lives forward. In the process of *shadow* incorporation, we start to recognise the unconscious part of ourselves as having the potential to be creative and inspirational as well as destructive.

This brings us to the notion that there are multiple but related domains of a person's self. Many of us would have experienced the occasional feeling that there is a voice inside us that feels like a monologue running inside our mind. For a depressed individual, he may experience a serious sounding, or a heavy voice being constantly active in his mental space, and filling it with ideas that make him feel sad. The heavy voice is often packed with words that tend to discourage him from experiencing a more powerful way of thinking, and from acting in his best interest. The voice may communicate ideas to him such as: "Your life is so boring and empty; you just do not belong anywhere," or "You are so useless; you can't do anything right." It is as though the depressed person is punishing himself for something. His self-respect disappears and his mind beats him to death with negative thoughts. This so-called inner voice is not an auditory hallucination. Rather, it is experienced as a stream of destructive thoughts towards himself.

At times, the voice appears to be an endless parade of comments about whatever the person is experiencing at the moment. When this commentary focuses on his own self, it can be a very negative impacting force on his life. At other times, there seems to be a continuous dialogue going on within him. This happens especially if someone has previously hurt him in some way and he enacts a scene of anger in his mind and envisions himself talking angrily. These dialogues can bring about a snowball effect, and when his emotions are evoked, he gets attached to them, worsening his anxiety.

We can also understand this inner voice by perceiving our unconscious mind as a composite structure of "different selves" interacting with each other. These different aspects of ourselves represent our ability to respond and adapt to different situations and different people. However, some of these adaptations are not always favourable to ourselves and we tend to suppress them as we grow into adults. So, when some of these selves appear, we may be a little surprised and wonder what to do with them. This perspective would help us to better appreciate the nature of the inner voice, or the way we organise the manner in which we experience different environmental circumstances in life.

There is, for instance, a part of our self that defines what we would like ourselves to be and how we wish to be seen by the world. This is the mask we wear, and we call this our *persona*. On the other hand, the *shadow* may be regarded as another part of our self, and it refers to that part of our unconscious mind that contains ideas, instincts, impulses, weaknesses, and embarrassing fears that have been hidden away. This more shady side of our inner psyche somewhat resembles the chaotic environment of the wilderness. Then, there is another part of ourselves that verbally narrates what is happening and attempts to make sense of what is going on around us. We can call this part our *narrator*, and this part describes our values and beliefs about the way the world works.

When a child is old enough to separate things and situations into good and bad, he starts to build his shadow self. In his interaction with others, he sorts out those traits within him that are socially unacceptable and hides them within this shadow. The shadow therefore contains the fear, anger and powerlessness

that are trapped within the person. The shadow self is also that part of him that feels separated from worthiness, security, wholeness and love. The reality is that our civilising process does not allow a person to reveal those aspects of him that do not fit in with the ideals of our society. Therefore, in learning to overcome depression, the person needs to recognise those personal characteristics and aspects of his life experiences that he has not been able to accept. These invariably involve his past wounds and losses.

During our growing phase, many of us have been mentally conditioned to assume that the fear, pain and insecurity within us are to be expected. They are just the way we have become because of the family we came from and what happened to us during our childhood. As a result, many of us may be aware of the existence of our wounds but stay stuck with them. The temptation is not to do anything but keep repeating our negative patterns of behaviour. When we feel powerless to overcome the force of these repetitive patterns in our lives, simply talking about our wounds may not be a sufficiently effective solution to the depression. Unless we dislodge and dissolve the painful emotions that are wedged in our unconscious mind, we remain stuck with the power the shadow has over us.

A common way of obstructing ourselves from healing is to deny that we have any feelings of anguish, suffering or anger. We are our own critic, and would not let ourselves shed tears. We tell ourselves that we are happy, and that stress and anger are non-existent within us. Many of us do not realise that a lot of the energy we use to repress our feelings is actually what makes us tired. If instead, we are able to let out our feelings and emotional tension, our life will become a whole lot easier. Otherwise, help from a psychotherapist may be necessary at this stage.

When we feel unworthy and believe that we are not being good enough, we are creating a false mental image of perfection. By accommodating this image of imperfection in our mind, we give credence to the voice in our head that puts us down. Let us continue to look at Rachel's example. She has been made to bear the blame for others at home or to suffer in their place since young, and this has created a feeling of unworthiness in her shadow self.

RACHEL ON EMOTIONAL HUNGER

Rachel has been desperately feeling the need to win her parent's trust and approval since early childhood. Her attempts to be loved, accepted and trusted have resulted in an eating disorder. Whenever a feeling of dissatisfaction arises, she tries to anaesthetise it by inappropriate eating.

Mum was really strict when I was young. She was the typical disciplinarian and would cane us whenever we misbehaved. Once, Mum told me not to touch the hot iron, but as a child I did anyway. I remember the skin peeling off my palms because it was so hot. However, instead of soothing and comforting me, Mum caned my wounds because she believed that when it hurts a lot, it would leave a lasting impression on me to never touch the hot iron again. That was the mantra she followed for raising both me and my sister.

Mum also used embarrassment as punishment. Almost every time we were out, she would scream at me or hit me in public with the warning: "I'm gonna make sure everyone knows what a bad girl you are." Her common favourite sentences to me were, "Why can't you walk faster? Are you trying to be vain by walking so slowly, like a prostitute?" And I remember when my sister misbehaved; she loved to call her an "animal". So we grew up really scared to report our injuries or pain because we knew we would get punished for them.

Mum also threatened me with her affection. Amidst her verbal name-calling, she would routinely shrug my hand away whenever I did something to upset her. Most of the time, I would not understand why what I did was wrong because she never explained. She would just say it was wrong, that she didn't want me anymore and that I was not worthy of love. Sometimes when she got too upset, she would leave me in the middle of the shopping mall and walk off.

As I was growing up, I was closer to my dad because Dad never once hit us. Mum and Dad quarrelled daily, and they still do today. So whenever Mum and Dad quarrelled, she would grumble to me and insult my dad, calling him a "bastard" and cursing him while forcing me to take sides. When I kept quiet and refused to insult my dad, she would scold me for siding him and betraying her efforts of raising me, and imply that I was hypocritical in my show of concern for her. I guess from all these early experiences, I started to develop this anxiety, that if I did not please people around me, I would be tossed away and

unworthy of love. So throughout my childhood, I never could handle expressions of emotions properly.

I also struggled a lot with my body image. My sister was a really fat baby and I grew up hearing my relatives talk about how concerned they were with her weight and size. My auntie was obsessed with dieting and being slim, and so I was terrified to be fat. Mum loved to dress me up, and she would dictate what I wore daily, even during my birthday parties. Many a time, this frustrated me a lot, because the clothes she selected made me look fat and I really didn't want to wear them. So whenever I was forced to wear clothes I didn't like, I would sit on the floor and rub my limbs against either the groove on the parquet or the ridges on the wall until I got friction burns or started to bleed.

Mum would also scoop heaps of rice whenever she fed us, because she believed that children should be chubby and fat. When I was 8 years old, I saw a documentary on eating disorders, meant to educate the public about the dangers of it and how to *seek treatment. I remember watching the girl on TV sticking her fingers down her throat after every meal to puke, in order to lose a lot of weight. So I learned, and each time my mother force-fed me, I would go and vomit it out. But it did not happen every day, only on days that I felt fat and unworthy of love.*

From Rachel's story, the notion of the shadow may be simplified into a bunch of painful emotions trapped within her. These emotions function to steer her to a behaviour that matches up to her painful self. Rachel's painful shadow is a reflection of her childhood insecurity of being unloved, her fear of growing fat and the risk of losing the needed approval from her mother. Unconsciously she feels the need to hold on to her pain in order to save herself for her future. The energy of her shadow self takes on a life of its own. Even though she disowns her shadow experience, represses it and does her best to prevent it from being brought to light, it turns out that the pain of her shadow shows up in its own terms with an even greater force, in the form of an eating disorder.

The more uncontrollable the stress we face in our life, the more likely we are to turn to food for emotional relief. Eating excessively to deny a deprivation of affection and nurturing relationships from early life is a common habit. Rachel is turning to emotional eating to fill her need for love. She is seeking the good-mother image in food and eating as an attempt to compensate for an immense unfulfilled need. It is like an insatiable desire for a love that is impossible.

The Nature of Depression

Life can be very different if each time we are feeling sad or angry as a kid, an adult comes and says to us, "Come dear; do tell me all about it. I am here to listen to you and be with you." As children, we all want our feelings to be welcomed with tenderness and our problems to dissolve.

Depression, in its pure form, is like giving up, a surrender. The sufferer takes on a posture of "I can't do it anymore", and over time, this evolves into the attitude of "I don't care even if I can't". Sometimes depression can be a struggling conflict between a desire and a moral injunction. One part of the individual is tempted to give up, while another part of him hangs on in a rebellious manner. Intertwined with the sense of hopelessness is the issue of guilt. The person may be tempted to give up because he suspects that the tragedy he is facing is caused by him. With time, he may just take the stance that he should stop struggling altogether because meaning has left him.

The opposite of depression is vitality, or the drive to do something every day in a person's life. For someone who has simply lost his vitality he would spend his weekends alone, uninterested in everything in his life, pretending to be tired and finding excuses for not doing anything at all. This is because the vitality in the person has shifted to that part of himself where he is struggling to resolve his inner conflicts. He would attempt to conceal his lethargy with smiles but often end up in a meaningless life situation.

Easing the Child's Heartache

Unlike adults who are capable of seeking help by themselves, teenagers rely heavily on adults to recognise their suffering and obtain the necessary help for them. Hence it is important for parents and teachers to spot the warning signs of depression early and take appropriate action. Instead of assuming that depressive symptoms are a normal part of the growing pains of adolescence, we should talk to our child about his fears and find out what is troubling him. Exploring his mood gently without getting emotional ourselves is the key. Even if we disagree with his perspectives and the reasons he gives, it helps to avoid being judgmental. It is good to make it clear to him that we will support him unconditionally regardless of his school performance. Refusing to do homework is a common behaviour, and in such a situation it is important that, as parents, we exercise control over our frustration and anger with him while communicating with his school teachers.

It is a reality that depressed young people often have many worries that they do not want to talk about. At a milder level, they may be just concerned about their external appearance and how others judge them. In more serious cases, like that of Rachel, they may be frequently disturbed by aches and pains that make them anxious that they might be suffering from a serious underlying illness. Asthmatic attacks are a common example of a medical illness that is linked with anxiety and depression and this is important for parents to be aware of.

Unfortunately, when depression in the irritable child manifests as anger or as moody behaviour directed at his parents, it is common for parents to react negatively and reciprocate. This would only create an emotional gap between them. In such a situation it is usually wiser for the parents to take a step back and explore the possible reasons behind the child's feelings and behaviour.

It is also a good idea for parents to spend enjoyable and relaxed time with their anxious and depressed child without discussing his troubled issues. Sometimes this may be difficult if the teenager is caught up with his own life and wants to be alone. Active listening is known to improve communication and helps young people feel that they are being cared for and understood. It involves dedicating time and undivided attention to listen to them when they feel like talking to us. It is not about figuring them out or evaluating their mental state to give them advice. It is about listening to them empathically and being able to feel the suffering that they are going through so that we acquire a better understanding of their concerns.

Parents often worry if listening too much to the teenager when he is upset would cause them to be more stuck in negative thoughts. I personally doubt if this would happen if the parents truly practice empathic listening. If they are able to understand and accept their children's worries, they would be in a better position to reassure them and more able to cheer them up from time to time. There is then little or no reason for their children to lapse into ruminative thinking.

As parents, we need to work on strengthening our relationship with our children beyond meeting their physical and material needs. It is common for teenagers to prefer their parents to stand off and not discuss conflict areas with them. This behaviour often puts the parents on the spot, but parents can still connect with their children through topics such as movies, novels, photography or sports or wherever there is a common interest. Such communication links can be fostered without attempting to slip into the deeper areas of the child's concern while waiting for him to open up emotionally.

Although teenagers may appear superficially not to care about their own problems, they usually need lots of encouragement from others in reality. Parents are the best people to highlight the positive aspects of their lives. Simple compliments about the good things they have done at home or in school would make a big difference to their self-image. It is human nature that we all like to be appreciated and recognised for doing something good, even if it is expected of us. It is important for the parents to make positive remarks when the child is trying harder at schoolwork or thank a child when he does a household chore.

It is also important to comment positively on any small signs of personal progress on his part, be it punctuality for the school bus or taking initiative to tidy up his own bedroom.

In the digital age, children are typically able to concentrate on computer games for hours on end, and yet encounter difficulty concentrating on their schoolwork. This usually frustrates and annoys parents, but there is a psychological reason underlying this behavioural tendency. The rapidly changing imagery on the computer screen provides a constant stimulation to the child's mind, and is unlike the unchanging appearance of the text in their school textbooks. For many of them, a sustained source of mental stimulus provides an escape route from their mental turmoil surrounding their schoolwork. Of course, this calls for balance.

Self-Management Tools

Young as they may be, there are effective ways for growing teenagers or maturing adolescents to help themselves avoid depression. The key is to develop self-reliance and learn to work things out for themselves. Even when they feel down, they should learn to push themselves to go to school and learn to enjoy their classroom studies. They need to focus on self-regulation and should not just passively allow things to happen to him. Rather, they should examine the situation, pick a strategy, evaluate whether things are working out as desired and reinforce their self-monitoring and self-control processes.

The most often talked about way for a young, troubled person to help himself is to share his own troubles with someone

else. The dictum, "A problem shared is a problem halved" is noteworthy. Teenagers and adolescents can spend time with friends and family members with whom they can talk to and make themselves feel good. Doing things with them will deepen bonds and allow them to feel supported. The fun that goes with sharing experiences with other people often makes them feel happier and more able to cope.

Another common way of coping is through distraction. Activities like going for a walk, exercising in the gym, cycling or playing a game are common examples. Physical exercise is a natural antidepressant and those exercises that involve a connection with nature would enhance the effect. For this reason, a walk in the park often makes a person feel relaxed, peaceful and grounded. So is listening to soothing music or doing something creative, like producing a piece of artwork.

Of course, it is not realistic for teenagers to escape from emptiness and anxiety by playing football or hanging out with friends all the time. Enjoying everyday experiences is great, but if used purely for avoiding emptiness, it may be insufficient for managing anxiety in the longer run. Engaging too much time in activities that do not help to build life skills are a waste of human energy. The person must learn to enjoy activities with increasingly complex goals, especially those goals that make meaning in their lives. He must also learn to ascribe meaning to events that normally produce monotony, boredom and despair. For instance, after an argument with his parents he should not brood over the situation but see the parent's point of view and how it relates to his own.

More important is the development of a personal meaning of life. Building one's life around goals derived from a personal setback or a tragedy often helps in cultivating resilience. When meaning is present in whatever one does, it is likely that the rest of his life will be in order. For example, a boy who has lost his parents while young may learn to volunteer his free time and offer his service for an orphanage. People who wish to fulfil their growth potential may choose to invest their energy in goals that are not just associated with their natural strengths but also with a purpose. It is a common observation that among those people who have discovered their life purpose, many have travelled abroad widely, spent extended time in the natural world or participated in a meaningful social change project.

I vividly recall an unexpected encounter with a bright, young lady in her early thirties in a remote village in Xinjiang a few years ago while I was travelling on the Silk Road in China. While enjoying the natural scenic beauty of this part of the country, I met this lady who had come alone all the way from her home in Hong

Kong for her sabbatical. She was spending her time interacting with the local Uigher residents in Xinjiang while finding meaning in life through helping out in a local village eatery. I was inspired when she told me of her plan to remain there for a further six months while reflecting on her purpose in life.

Experiencing depression is not necessarily bad if a person can perceive it as a valuable phase of his life journey instead of a mental illness. A depressive episode may sometimes be a turning point in one's life where soul-searching is called for. Our priorities, values, self-image and directions need to be re-evaluated at certain points in our life. It is during such times that we need people to understand us, and we should not be feeling ashamed of our emotional pain as we respond to our own suffering with self-love, respect and clarity.

When a person is depressed, what he requires is not to eliminate his suffering, but to regain his *wholeness*. In truth, suffering is an unavoidable facet of human life. We have been brought up to equate happiness with an elimination of suffering. We thus overlook the fact that true happiness includes suffering as part of our mental state. We need to distinguish happiness from the feeling of enjoyment that we derive from entertainment or material pleasure. True happiness is a state of inner peace and fulfilment that is long-lasting and deeply satisfying. It broadens our mental outlook, deepens our love for each other and survives even when times are tough. It grows through hardship and struggle and is at its peak when we are able to give and receive unconditional love. It is also the reason for us to continue living.

LUCY ON MENTAL SILENCE IN MANAGING DEPRESSION

Mindfulness and contemplation are powerful tools for managing suffering. Lucy, who has had suicidal thoughts since the age of six, has been suffering from severe attacks of muscle pains from fibromyalgia, a chronic musculoskeletal disorder. She shares with me how she uses mental stillness, love and mindfulness as a way to manage her depression, while maintaining her clarity of purpose.

When I am not in pain, I indulge in silence. Silence somehow makes me feel like I am in a different dimension where I can feel the love, compassion and a healing effect. However, when I am in severe pain, I always develop anxiety as if my soul would be taken away soon. During such moments, I usually need a close one to keep me company and to reassure me that I still exist.

I had an experience yesterday where I knew I was going to get frustrated as I was irritated by the TV volume. I managed to put my reactive anger on hold and got myself out of the house to a nearby park.

During the walk, I maintained my mindfulness. I focused inwards and observed the feeling of a ball of fiery energy within, but at the same time without reacting to it or actively resisting its eruption. When I reached the park, I surrendered myself to nature and the ball of energy diffused to the surroundings from all parts of my body. It was such a blissful moment as the pent-up energy was being released and I found my mind dancing with the flow of nature again. I believe this experience has taught me deeply on how to manage difficult feelings in the future.

Instead of eliminating anger and irritation, Lucy sought inner peace through a mindfulness approach. From her story, we get a glimpse of the contentedness of one's joy through attaining the state of *wholeness*. Seeking to be whole means seeking to improve one's abilities and balance one's mental state. It requires that a person live up to his highest potential in all aspects of living. The concept of being whole spans the entire human experience from intellectual rationality, morality, cultural norms and physical health to emotional stability and human spirituality. It involves the union of the unconscious with the conscious mind and one's harmony with the natural world.

The conventional medical paradigm of depression tends to be biological in orientation, and is attributed to a "chemical imbalance" in the brain as a major contributory cause. Correcting this imbalance by restoring brain chemistry has become the widely articulated basis for using antidepressant medication to elevate moods. The wholeness perspective, on the other hand, encompasses a broader scope and is based on the premise that the neurochemical imbalance is a fraction of a broader disequilibrium between the mind (psyche) and the body (soma). This psychosomatic imbalance is perceived to have come about as a result of beliefs and assumptions that have distorted one's self-image and undermined one's self-confidence. This allows symptoms of headaches, insomnia, muscular pains and allergic skin reactions to appear. The wholeness approach works by helping a person to question his unspoken assumptions and this involves the application of certain foundational concepts.

Firstly, the growing adolescent needs to clarify his aspirations in each moment of his life. He has to ask himself what he considers the most important thing in his life and what he values the most. He needs to contemplate on the meaning and purpose of life as he searches within. Life unfolds along the lines of what he values most and it is important that no one else defines his aspirations for him. After clarifying his aspirations, he must follow them through and this requires clarity on his part as to what he is willing to take on and what he is prepared to give up. With clarity, the act of following through his aspirations can become a powerful force in his life that helps him to develop the needed resilience to survive hostile life circumstances. Whatever he chooses to do, he has to take responsibility for himself because his life belongs to him and not someone else.

Sincerity with oneself is absolutely essential for this step of his journey. It encompasses the qualities of honesty, genuineness and integrity and allows him to see himself as he is, with all his imperfections. He must not be held captive by his conditioned mental assessment of himself. To be a good steward of his life journey, he has to refrain from running away from the troubling aspects of his day-to-day life. Withdrawing into denial and avoiding challenges will not lessen his sufferings. When he is prepared to face whatever comes along and give each moment the attention and commitment it deserves, he will be able to see his entire life as the path to realising the truth about himself. At each step of the journey, he has to learn to pause and reflect to understand why he needs to pay attention to what his life events are trying to tell him.

Often the adolescent has been conditioned by adults during his upbringing to accept that hate, dishonesty and greed are an indispensable part of everyone's life. With this mindset, he is inclined to continue to justify the reality of what is causing him emotional pain and finds himself trapped in an environment of conflict, strife and fear. He feels like being exiled to the shadow realm of his silent anguish while believing that this is perfectly rational. Deep down, he may sense that something is wrong with the way he looks at life but still chooses to ignore it. It is like living behind a veil that obscures him from self-awareness and from seeing his own relationship with his life.

Mindfulness meditation makes a good mental mirror. To be mindful simply means to be aware and focused on oneself and one's feelings in the present without being judgmental about them. Meditation is the art and practice of seeing everything as they are in the deepest possible way while maintaining mental quietness. When meditation is performed in a mindful fashion, it helps the individual to let go of personal will and not seek happiness through control and striving. With continual

practice, he will learn to let go of his effort to control and stop manipulating his life experiences.

Mindfulness meditation familiarises our mind with positivity. The more familiar we are with positivity, the quieter and more peaceful we would feel. When we are free from mental discomfort, we will begin to experience calmness and happiness. If we can train our mind to maintain inner peace and tranquillity, we will feel wholesome and happy all the time, even under difficult conditions.

The mental silence and stillness achieved via mindfulness meditation is the bedrock upon which we can build our inward stability, objectivity and non-attachment. These are natural antidotes against anxiety. I have provided details of the mindfulness technique and anecdotal experience in my previous book, *Bend Not Break*. The basic principle of the practice of mindfulness is to cultivate the attitude of surrender, effortlessness and openness and the basic technique is to maintain awareness of the present moment with acceptance. This enables us to make a commitment to something other than our restless mind.

When we meditate we are not spending the time to figure out our problems or to analyse our past experiences. Nor are we fighting with our mind to make it quiet. Rather, we are letting insights emerge from the depths of our inner calm. In the early stages of starting meditation we need to tame our mind like the way we would tame a wild horse. Our thoughts tend to run wild and we need to allow time for our consciousness to adapt to the torrent of thoughts emerging from the subconscious. Our thoughts are just transient phenomena passing through our awareness. Just as we would watch clouds pass by in the sky, we let our thoughts come and go during the meditative process without judging or reacting to them. Once we get the feel of the technique, we will be able to concentrate on the silent gaps between these thoughts and start building our platform of inner calm.

Many a time, past painful memories may arise during meditation. When that happens, simply allow them to surface without analysing or reacting to them. Let them pass and fade off. Such memories do not define who we are but are merely pockets of unconscious energy that comes to our conscious awareness to be purified before being released from our system. These painful memories often evoke and bring forth questions about one's life and reasons for suffering. Finding answers to them requires meditative inquiry.

Inquiry is an attitude of curiosity that lives within us and represents our desire to know the truth. This can be done by surrendering to the silence and stillness achieved during mindfulness. By questioning our assumptions and beliefs and holding the question in silent waiting, it opens our mind for intuitive wisdom to surface. The art of meditative inquiry goes beyond the power of the intellectual mind and bypasses our childhood conditioning. The quiet and stillness of the mind enables us to come forth with answers to address the deepest existential issues that confront our human self.

There are two aspects of the inquiry process, the first of which is to take a step back and remove our self from all prior conditioned thinking. This makes way for a realisation of the truth. There is no necessity to actively search for answers in the meditative state because they will spontaneously surface from the mental stillness. We may want to ask questions like: "Who am I? How accurate is my Story of Self?" or "What is the reason for doing what I am doing now?" We need to take our time to trace the thread of questioning about all the beliefs about our self and the hidden assumptions about who and what we are.

The second aspect of inquiry involves accessing the clarity and wisdom that is housed in the stillness at the root of our consciousness. Our wisdom tends to flow out as an "Aha" moment of great insight. All we need to do is to simply receive and embrace the insight with gratitude and let that insight stay with us. We all have a Story of Self that communicates the key formative experiences that have shaped the way we think who we are. After accessing our intuitive wisdom, we need to contemplate on our self-narrative.

Contemplation is the art of holding a statement in the silence and stillness of awareness until it begins to disclose deeper meaning and understandings. It transcends analytical thought and opens up our consciousness to reveal new insights. For example, if we hold the phrase "I am not my story" in our awareness when we contemplate, we will learn to realise how and why we have been creating a particular self-narrative that has handicapped ourselves all along.

It is when we ruminate over who we think we are, and how we have been suffering, that we begin to unconsciously heighten our anxiety to depressive levels. We may want to hold a second statement in the stillness of our mind: "Suffering occurs when we believe in a thought that is at odds with what actually is." Contemplating this statement may awaken us to the fact that life can be lived from a re-conditioned state of mental being. Once we accept the truth about our selves, we begin to appreciate the fact that the key to freedom from depression is actually in our hands.

 LUCY ON CONTEMPLATION AND MEDITATION

Lucy, who has lost her job recently, went through a period of depression while she was struggling with her chronic fatigue syndrome. However, she gradually recovered from it as she contemplated the life path she was taking.

I thought that after leaving my workplace, I would finally experience peace. I was wrong. The confrontation with the self is as tedious as facing the external environment. There were a lot of adjustments, physically, mentally, emotionally and spiritually, as is common in a major switch in life. There were ups and downs I faced. Finally having time of my own was the most precious thing ever. I still went for classes, so I was not completely cut off from society. I finally had no more stress from my work, research and ex-boss. These areas had previously affected me tremendously.

I finally had time to read things I enjoy and time to meditate and heal myself. One night, as I was in a deep contemplative state, I felt like I was an onion peeling off layer by layer, and the layers represented all the masks, inauthenticity and delusive perspectives which I had put on as I worked in society. As the layers peeled off, I felt where I was exactly, my true self. It made me reflect that when we put ourselves in society, there are so many imaginary roles we have to play just to meet up to general expectations and standards. These layers are heavy and I hope to shed more of these as I meditate further.

As my true self is revealed to me day by day, I am truly confronting myself. There are a lot of "who am I" questions. I can wake up with anxiety or a lot of energy arising for no reason. Fortunately, I have past experiences of anxiety to help me be calm enough to face these sensations. Rather than suppress these forces, I just have to accept their presence and let them come through. I question why I have symptoms of pain and fatigue whenever I encounter difficulties. There are people who have recovered from chronic fatigue syndrome. We have *to build strength in ourselves in whichever dimension we are weak in and move on. People who suffer physically like me tend to look forward to a closure to our lives. However, it seems like there is no closure until we find the particular space in which we feel a sense of belonging.*

Eliminating depression may involve the awakening of an intelligence that is born of our inner silence. The inner silence has the ability to uproot the old structures of our consciousness and provide us with a creative thought. This is done by leveraging on the stillness created during meditation. The technique used is that of *creative visualisation*. The latter is the art of creating mental images of whatever situation we desire. This purposeful process of generating mental imagery simulates a visual perception. As we get into a meditative state with the eyes closed, we can maintain, examine or transform the generated imagery to modify our level of emotional pain or sense of self-worth. This approach works at the level of the unconscious mind and expedites our healing.

A good example of someone who uses creative visualisation to help people see examples of the dream they wish will come true is Walt Disney. He has done it in the context of an entertainment business, but the principles of creating happiness are the same. While we are in a meditative state, it is common for our unconscious mind to spontaneously generate specific imagery that is associated with anxious moments of our past. By intentionally altering these recollected images of distressing events and replacing them with imagery that precipitates comfort, harmony, happiness, we can initiate emotional change.

The theoretical basis behind creative visualisation is that of symbolic thinking. The unconscious mind does not make a difference between what is real and what is vividly imagined. Nor does it make a difference between what is real danger and the feeling of being in danger. If we direct our unconscious mind to experience positive feelings, we will start feeling better both physically and emotionally. By visualising the kinds of things that we would like to do, whom we like to do them with, we will find that our life begins to change. This technique has a major application in psychotherapy but is also a tool that we can learn to use and practice by our self, as Lucy has shown by her example:

While struggling to get out of her depressive state after losing her job, Lucy faced a double whammy when she was suddenly hit with a food allergy. She approached me for help while at the same time sourcing for medical experts in allergy. I taught her the use of creative visualisation in combination with personification, a technique of assigning human qualities to inanimate objects or abstract notions.

 ## LUCY ON CREATIVE VISUALISATION

In her meditative state Lucy was able to visualise her food allergy in the form of a personified image that appeared like a "genie". She was able to quieten her mind and interact with this genie. The message from the genie was that the food allergy was part of a learning process that she had to go through as a hurdle in her life. Her depression had come about because of the hurt she experienced from other people's criticisms about her.

> *I knew what the image was trying to tell me. It was time I was firm with who I was, and be myself. I am pretty self-affirming. I enjoy being a calm, quiet person. However, when I think about having to face people who are not on the same frequency as me, I start to feel anxious, with some degree of anger.*
>
> *For instance, in my current part-time job, I have been ostracised by people. I do not converse much and just do what I am assigned to do quietly at one corner, but this working style seems like a kind of "sin" in that working environment. There is a clear message that I did not belong in this workplace and people wanted me to leave. I feel very saddened that I am not given the opportunity to be myself in this environment. I really want to leave the job as I can't tolerate the very hurtful conversations, badmouthing and cursing. But at the same time, I wish to earn enough to support myself. I truly do not want to rely on my family anymore. It's time to get out and lead a normal working life.*

One of the powerful lessons that Lucy learned from this contemplative experience is that her life potential lies beyond the power of her past and it can only blossom when she is not held hostage by her past experiences. Beyond her conditioned mind is her sacred self which allows her life to blossom. By repeatedly sending positive images to her mind, and visualising herself as living a normal and happy life that is filled with exciting adventures and great friends, she has since found a powerful way of fighting her anxiety and loving herself to get out of depression.

Chapter 2

Meeting Young Peoples' Emotional Needs

THE world of parenting lies in uncharted waters and is ripe with life lessons. Fundamentally, to be able to take care of a child well, parents must take advantage of the available opportunities to learn to love the child unconditionally. Unfortunately, the word and notion of "love" is often misunderstood and remains a mystery to many people.

Love starts from the moment a woman accepts her role as the mother of a child and expands her emotions from there. To love a child is to consistently meet the child's physical and emotional needs as appropriate. Only through a deep emotional connection and nurturance would a parent be able to work towards developing a lifetime's bond with his child.

What is Unconditional Love?

Parental love is the first love a child experiences, understands and treasures because it makes all the difference in his growth process. Unconditional love from parents is the kind of love they show to their kids for who they are and not for what they do. In essence, it is a combination of the human elements of kindness, helpfulness, sympathy, commitment and compassion and which requires unselfish acts and forgiveness to help in its delivery.

Loving others unconditionally is the act of extending our self into an uncharted emotional territory with the belief that we want to benefit another person regardless of the outcome. It is a pure act of generosity and selflessness and may not be intuitive to many of us. This is because we have been mentally programmed by our social environment to expect something in return for the love we dispense to others. We have learned to be conditional in our relationships to give love only when others reciprocate and have overlooked that true love is about caring for the happiness of another person without thinking of the return.

 Love is no longer unconditional when other people like us for doing what they want, because in this situation we are just paying a price to get their attention. Unconditional love is shown when people do not feel disappointed or irritated with us

even when we fail to do what they want of us. It is this love alone that has the power to generate great relationships and heal all wounds.

A word of caution is needed here. Unconditional love does not mean that we accept our child's inappropriate behaviour blindly. However, we still do love our children even at those times when we dislike their behaviour. Getting children out of the trouble they have caused for themselves and assisting them repeatedly to avoid the consequences of their bad decisions is not love. True love is about letting a child learn his life's lessons the hard way, while at the same time letting him know that we are there for him when he needs help.

Real love never fails even when tested to the limit. It continues unabated even when the parents are frustrated and their patience is tested by their children. It is important for young people to be aware that they are really loved by their parents if they are to avoid depression. The reason is simple. Whenever a child feels loved, he has the strength to weather the crises that come his way. This is the basis of developing resilience as described in my previous book, *Bend Not Break*.

In the early stages of parenting, loving the child unconditionally is simple. The newborn baby is adorable and charming to the mother and brings happiness to all family members including the grandparents. The innocent infant has neither words to argue against the parents nor any behaviour to defy them. However the feeling of mutual love changes as the parent-child relationship grows and continues to evolve.

In the teenage years, the balance of exchange is tilted towards fulfilling the emotional needs of the child. In return, the parent gets satisfaction from his successes and achievements in school. The motive is to work towards a mutually satisfying relationship.

Some parents love their child with an unvoiced expectation that the child will support them in their old age. Hence, they feel let down eventually when this does not happen. They rue the fact that they went out of their way to bestow their love and that the child has neglected his duty of meeting their expectations. However, true love cannot be dispensed like a bank loan waiting to be repaid.

Unconditional love involves meeting not only the material needs but also the emotional needs of the child. When we love our child for who he is and who he will become, we are not disappointed or hurt when he is thoughtless or gives us nothing back in return. For the child who receives parental love, each moment of unconditional acceptance creates a living thread that weaves the connection between him and the parent who accepts him. When he is aware that his family members love him unconditionally, he feels a similar connection with everyone else in society.

Family Love

The family is where life begins and love emanates. From the moment of birth the infant personality is being shaped by the intimacy of the mother-child relationship. The love between the parent and the child is mutual. Each of them desires the other's love and yearns for it. The infant instinctively clings on to his mother who constantly cuddles and smiles at him. Out of this close bonding, the child's individuality gradually separates from the emotional togetherness of the relationship as he grows.

The manner in which parents show their love for one another and for their child shapes the emotional climate of the family. The growing child will love both parents when he senses that his parents love each another. If the parents hate one another, the child will feel compelled to take sides and turn fearful of losing the love of one parent in favour of the other. This creates anxiety.

There are unfortunate situations when the loving environment is absent from birth. If a woman becomes a parent against her will or if she wants a son but gets a daughter, she may wish that the newborn baby never existed. Under such circumstances, the parent dislikes the child even if she continues to feed and clothe him.

Occasionally parents find it difficult to accept their child who comes to them as an unpleasant surprise. For example if a child is born with a congenital hearing defect, the parents must accept his defect completely if they are to love the child, and able to talk about it to other parents without getting emotionally upset. As another example, parents who are of a high educational standing and discover that their child is only of average intelligence must accept the child's intellectual status if they are to love the child.

When parents love their children, they see them as intrinsically good in themselves. Children also have a right to their parents' love. The parents will provide their children with those things to which they are entitled, simply because they love them. They may at times grumble at the loss of freedom which they used to enjoy before the birth of the child, or complain about the high cost of things which their child needs, but this does not mean they do not love them. They will still buy for them. When parents supply their children with the necessary things, the child does not owe their parents anything. Each generation receives from the previous generation and pays out for the next generation.

Self-Love

Unconditional love in any relationship starts with oneself. The individual must have a strong sense of self-esteem and self-confidence to begin with. He must generally feel good about himself, like himself and recognise the positive qualities that he can bring to a relationship. He remains fully himself even when he is together with someone else and he does not need another person to define who he is. Loving himself will then provide him with the strength of heart and mind to love another individual in the same way.

Loving oneself unconditionally means that he is able to view himself as being worthy of love despite his past mistakes and perceived deficiencies. A person knows his own flaws and shortcomings better than anyone else. Being able to love oneself despite knowing his own faults paves the way for him to offer the same to others. For this reason he must be able to accept and forgive his own imperfections in order to do the same for someone else.

Self-love is neither synonymous with self-interest nor with selfishness. Loving oneself is primarily self-acceptance, and the pursuit of one's self-interest is secondary. Everyone has physical or intellectual inadequacies of some sort, like a short stature or a deficiency in artistic skills. Occasionally, the inadequacy may be psychological, such as a fear of blood. Hence, if an adolescent aspires to be a medical student, it may be difficult for him to accept the reality. Yet, if he is able to abandon his ambition to enter medical school and explore other career opportunities, he is loving himself.

Self-love requires a person to be satisfied to be the kind of person he is. In the previous chapter, Carol's tenacity and persistence in pursuing her ambition and a career in the landscape industry despite her limiting medical condition illustrates how non-acceptance of one's inadequacy, or lack of self-love, could aggravate mental agony and worsen depression when she was frustrated with repeated rejections. These feelings of rejection sting because our brain is wired to respond to rejection similarly to the way it responds to physical pain. Some people sustain deeper emotional wounds than others from such incidents of rejection, and this can add to the negativity in their character. Sometimes, even a mere look or a harmless comment can be interpreted as a true rejection and add on to the person's anxiety.

The Child's Emotional Needs

To feel loved, every child needs a security base from which he can venture into the outside world, and to which he can safely return with physical and emotional nourishment awaiting him. He needs comfort when he is distressed and reassurance if he is frightened. As parents and caregivers, we have to remain available and stay ready to respond whenever we are called upon to provide encouragement or intervention when necessary.

Parental love is the first condition of the child's security. However, this can be considerably weakened if there is no harmony between parents. Marriage break-ups of parents affect young children in the same way as their rejection by parents. When a man separates from his wife, the child is likely to feel that the father has left him rather than left the mother, and that the fault lies with him because he is unworthy of the father's love.

As the child gets older, he ventures steadily further away from his base for increasing durations of time and gradually learns to build his own security base in a world beyond the home. However, if a person is not brought up on a solid foundation of love, he tends to stay immersed in uncertainty and in a zone of insecurity in his adult life. There are times when the parents' marriage is falling apart and the child is told that he is a burden and made to feel that his needs have no place in the family. In such a case, the child may get a sense that he is a living burden to the family and unworthy of the attention and love of his family members.

BRENDA ON CHILDHOOD SECURITY AND ANXIETY

Some years ago, Brenda came to ask for help with regards to managing her depression. She broke into tears the moment she started recollecting her memories of her parents' discord and her emotions of childhood insecurity.

Dad has had an extramarital affair since I was young. We stayed in our grandfather's property until I was four and then we moved to an apartment. Then, this lady half-moved in with us. I don't know how my mum took it. They always locked the room, and the three of them would quarrel, cry, and even shout inside. As kids we were curious and put our ears to the door but I didn't understand what was going on then.

The situation became so bad that this woman started to pry open my dad's car and damage the door. Finally my dad broke off with her and wanted to divorce my mum. My mum wouldn't agree to it because she said she and her two children would have nowhere else to go.

I felt that I could not leave my family. Whenever I walked into the house, there was so much tension that I felt I should just move out and grow up on my own. But I couldn't. I have always found excuses like, "Oh my parents need me," or "What if my dad disowns me?" So I stayed with them until I was in my late thirties.

The doctor diagnosed me as co-dependent because my mum has been depressed for as long as I know and I find myself having to take care of her. She is always having headaches, always crying and always gambling. I can't tell my dad the truth and I have to lie for her or keep quiet.

My mum hates me despite what I've done for her. She would hit me and say, "I hate you to the bones." Then she would start this joke about me and say I was actually that woman's kid. My brother also hates me. My mum once said, crying, that I was picked up from the dustbin. She wouldn't send me to school or pick me after school, and my brother would have to do that

instead. I was really scared, because he was always late. Once I was alone in school and there was no one around in the whole estate for an hour, and I was only four or five then.

For the child who wants to feel loved, being given the opportunity to grow is another important emotional need. To many parents this need is less obvious as compared with the need for security. They tend to think that as long as they can keep their child safe at home, growth will follow automatically.

The first four to five years in a child's life constitute the foundational period that shapes the child's learning achievements and happiness. A caring and supportive environment paves the way for his transition from home to school. Without being given the freedom to grow during his maturation phase, the child tends to break away from home and seek freedom for himself. Should this happen, he will have to struggle with the immaturities of youth which he may not recognise at his age.

The attachment pattern the individual develops during his growing years is significantly influenced by the way his parents treat him. If he is confident that his parent will be available and responsive in the event of a frightening situation he will feel bolder in exploring the outside world. Otherwise, in the absence of certainty, he tends to become more prone to separation anxiety, more clinging and more anxious about exploring the world. If he expects to be rebuffed whenever he asks for help, he may decide to live his life without the love of others.

Another major emotional need of the child who wants to feel loved is that of a concrete personal ideal. This ideal is embodied in the child's earliest conception of what he would like to be and often built on parental models. Typically, the ideal takes the form of a strong father and a tender loving mother, and the image of what they do and say are all absorbed into the consciousness of the child as desirable features and determines his vision of himself.

However, the mere presence of an ideal does not insure that it is emulated. If the ideal is not commensurate with his own potential, he may waste his youth hopelessly striving and failing to discover his own abilities. If the child has very able parents, he may feel the pressure to succeed along parental lines. This can steer him into making attempts in which defeat and discouragement is inevitable. It is therefore important to have parents who make good companions, prepared to listen to the child's ideals and prevent him from drifting into aimlessness.

When parents understand a child's needs, listen empathically to his ideals and consider his potentials, the child can connect better with them. Advice given by the parents is generally ineffective if they do not take the trouble to get root of the thinking that underlies the child's ideals. A growing child with an evolving identity needs a safety valve to air his views without which he is unlikely to be receptive to the views offered to him by adults. If the parents are not authoritative and their suggestions are unobtrusive, their views are more likely to be accepted. For those parents who are aware of their own deficiency in life skills, they may not want to act as a model but can still play the role of a guide for the child.

Parental Expectations

A natural component of parental love is the desire to see the child succeed. Since the educational field is the main area in which most children can distinguish themselves, educational ideals appear to be the commonest stumbling block for parental pride. As academic standards are easily quantifiable, high exam scores have become a symbol of superiority and are believed to correlate closely with success in adult life. When parents are concerned for the child's academic achievements more to satisfy their own ideals than for the child's sake, a major problem is being created. In the event that the child fails to attain the goals of his ambition, he may be psychologically thwarted by the parent's attitude in his next stage of development.

Two types of parental attitudes are known to have a negative impact on their children. At one extreme, the parents would want no let downs on the continuity of the family line. When an elder child in the family makes a brilliant academic record, they would find it difficult to accept anything less from a younger child. When the younger child fails to measure up to expected family standards, the parents are often puzzled and fail to recognise that their achievement anxiety over the child influences his emotional state and works against his future accomplishment.

On the other extreme, if a parent herself has been denied the opportunity for educational advancement in his younger days, she may focus her hope on the child to carry her ideals on to fulfilment. She does not realise that she is using the child for her personal ends instead of what is best for the child himself. All may go well if the child performs well. However, if the child refuses to align with the parent's plan, he risks precipitating a family tragedy. By disappointing his parent's ideals and hurting the family pride, he may be regarded as being non-filial for failing to give the parents a due return on investment. He may even become an object of dislike in the family. Worst still, the child may have to spend a greater part of his lifetime to overcome the guilt for having failed the parents' expectations.

Loneliness and Solitude

To be with others is a basic human need. Teenagers are usually at their lowest mood when they are alone, away from family, school or friends. Passive activities performed in solitude, such as watching TV or movies online or reading novels tend not to be the kind that makes them very happy, nor have much impact on their self-development.

Loneliness is a feeling of discomfort of not being connected with others in a meaningful way. A person feels lonely largely because he does not see or talk to anyone very often nor does he feel understood or cared for even when he is among people. He does not share any of his life challenges with people who care. Some lonely people are desperate for love but don't know how to go about finding it. Loneliness often goes hand in hand with depression. Depressed people often describe the bleakness of their mental state they experience without the cushion of love, how they would avoid the world and their feeling of isolation, even at crowded parties.

Loneliness is reduced by the company and emotional energy of other people that helps to keep the individual in a balanced mental state. Having close meaningful relationships is essential to our well-being. When we feel cut off from the people around us, we become more susceptible to anxiety and depression. People tend to cope with loneliness in different self-defeating ways. Rachel has described, in Chapter 1, how she would indulge in food to fill the void that comes with being deprived of a meaningful connection with her family members.

Loneliness is different from solitude. Loneliness refers to a painful feeling whereas solitude is a self-expression of the pride  and glory of being alone. In solitude, the person chooses to be alone, wants that aloneness and is comfortable with it. However, this may not necessarily be a good thing because it can predispose a maturing child to a feeling of emptiness. Over time, anxiety or despair sets in because the child feels separated from a secure base. Typically, children who have been sent away to a boarding school in a foreign land for long periods are potential candidates for depression in later life.

Not many people are prepared to admit to being lonely. Those who seek help from the doctor would do so with regards to his anxiety or depression but rarely divulge their feeling of loneliness. Our society takes the view that if a person does not have friends, there is something intrinsically wrong with him. He must be unapproachable, selfish or simply weird. For the same reason, school kids would prefer to hide their loneliness to avoid being judged as unlikeable.

Feeling lonely does not always mean that a person feels deprived of all relationships. Rather, he may feel unhappy about particular aspects of relationships. He may have supportive parents and yet feel lonely because the parents spend too much time at work. When the feelings of loneliness lead to anger or depression, the family members may find his depression confusing and the child himself may not realise that loneliness has an impact on his depression.

The opposite of loneliness is closeness. Closeness is reflected in mutual feelings of trust and respect and enables people to work cooperatively within a family or a community. Beyond the need to be aware of the presence of others, there is also the need to feel that one is being heard, seen, felt and taken notice of. Even more important, a person appreciates being wanted, liked and valued because he gets a sense of his own reality out of what others say to him and think about him.

Relating is the act of giving closeness to others. There are several ways in which closeness can be given, such as doing something pleasant to someone or being listened to. Often times, closeness involves the participants behaving as though they were part of a community. This happens when they share living space, possessions, activities, feelings, ideas, values and hopes. The most satisfactory close relations are usually those in which each partner sometimes gives and sometimes receives and when neither partner is conscious of who is the giver or who the receiver is. Despite the popularity of social media these days, substituting real-life interactions with online communications does not generate the same level of desired closeness.

Wanting to understand and know about another person is another form of closeness. When people become close they often vow that they will keep no secrets from each other. However, there is a need for a person to have a firm sense of self-identity before he can safely enter into such a close relationship with another. Otherwise, his identity becomes absorbed into that of the partner and every other relationship risks a further loss of his self-identity.

The insecure person who lacks a clear self-identity usually has a problem with closeness. He either chooses to avoid close

relationship altogether or becomes dependent on the other person for his own being. Avoidance of closeness does not mean that he does not care. It is largely a biological reaction that is ingrained in the mind through certain parenting practices in childhood. If he becomes totally identified with the other person he adopts all his values, beliefs and opinions. In contrast, the secure individual is able to relate one way with one person and another way with another. This is an important skill to acquire if an adolescent is going to survive in a loveless family.

Growing Up in a Loveless Environment

All lasting relationships require unconditional love and this includes family relationships. To further appreciate unconditional love, let us examine the dynamics of a loveless family, in which the anxiety levels are high. A loveless family can appear in different forms. A child may be raised by a single parent or fostered out to someone else. His parents could be separated, divorced or remarried. He may be in the company of half-siblings or step-siblings. Someone in his family could be an alcoholic, a drug addict or have gone to prison. In the worst case scenario, he could have been abused by his caregiver in early childhood. Yet, a loveless family can still exist without all these factors.

Some parents choose not to love their child at all. For instance, if a woman has become a parent against her will she may, after giving birth, wish that the child has not come the world in the first place. As another example, if a mother wants a son but gets a daughter, she may wish that the baby girl had never been born.

Growing up in a loveless family poses many problems to the

growing child in later adulthood. One common problem is a difference between how a parent or a sibling sees the child, and how the child sees himself. This sows the seed for developing anxiety and depression since the internal turmoil generated will prevent the child from connecting with his family members. No matter how he represses his hurt feelings, anger and fear will continue to creep back into his life.

Sometimes an adolescent may find that his family refuses to accept facts about his life or is unable to forgive him for something he considers very ordinary. For instance, he may dislike Mathematics and have low scores for that subject in school while all his other siblings excel in that subject. He may have ignored his parents' advice on the choice of university course. He may have dated someone from a different religious background or a different nationality. He may choose to listen to songs and music that his parents consider to be of bad taste. All these could make his family members dislike him.

Sometimes the situation is more emotionally shattering. He may have been told by his parents that they have given birth to him by mistake, and regretted having conceived him. He may have gone hungry during school hours with his parents not bothering if he has sufficient pocket money to buy food. He may be sick and family members respond casually by saying, "Oh, but you are fine now." Family members only pass sarcastic remarks at him. They ignore or downplay his achievements and may choose to shatter his spirit out of jealousy. They belittle him despite his achievements because they want to maintain their preconceived image of him as the person they believe he is supposed to be. The list goes on.

In the absence of love, family members may be superficially polite and supportive to each other but deep down they are disconnected and distanced by jealousy. When a sibling relationship is founded on competition instead of love, resentment builds up. Many of us are raised with the moral value that "blood is thicker than water" and this unfortunately steers us into perceiving put-downs by other family members as a necessary part of affection and growing up. However, when parents and siblings become overly mean-spirited, it becomes increasingly clear to the individual that love is not existent in the family. He may then start to find ways to dissociate from the family as he gets older.

 RACHEL ON THE LOVELESS FAMILY

Rachel continues with her story of how she batttled her mounting depression while living with her loveless family during her growing-up years.

My sister and I have stopped talking to each other for two years until recently when our relationship improved. I don't go home every single day, and I don't go home early. I usually reach home at 11.45 pm when everyone is asleep. The situation is so bad that even when I am done with my errands outside and I reach home early, I will stand outside the front door but am unable to bring myself to walk in if I know that everyone at home is still awake. I will just go down to the void deck instead and loiter around till 11.45 pm by which time everyone would have been asleep.

I am avoiding not just my sister alone, but my whole family. I think my sister will get very hurt if she hears this, but deep down I think she already knows. Recently, things have improved a bit and I would go home at least once a week.

The whole family is weird, and I have grown up in a melodramatic type of environment. My mum is super-dramatic. She has a lot of issues herself. She is hot-tempered and angry and self-victimises a lot. She has taken a knife and threatened to hack my sister. When I was young, it was a daily thing, and everybody would be fighting every day.

My sister was very violent when I was young. I was the quiet one and I would give in to everybody. So I was very scared every time when I came home and saw everybody screaming and shouting at each other. They were always fighting. A few years ago, my sister was so bad that she threatened to punch my mum and my mum almost sent her to the Girl's Home. It was that dramatic.

Sibling-Related Problems

When a parent is particularly devoted to one child or especially disappointed in him, the others in the family are usually affected by it. The parents themselves seldom admit their act of favouritism, and likewise, the children tend to deny the existence of jealousy between them and put up a front of solidarity. Sibling love and sibling jealousy are conflicting emotions and see-sawing between the two would result in a love-hate relationship in the long run.

In a loveless family, the older sibling is often more interested in showing off his talents and proving his superiority. He may vent his frustrations out on the younger sibling or tell his younger  sibling things that would traumatise him. The latter may face a lot of difficulty making sense of life, figuring out how to live or what to believe. Despite his bitterness the other family members may force him to reconcile with the elder sibling. Little by little, he would decide to estrange from all his family members.

Some parents would significantly change their expression of love towards a child when a new baby arrives and fail to see the underlying danger in this behaviour. In transferring most of their love to the newcomer, they potentially create jealousy and invite antagonism from an elder sibling. The child feels that he is being displaced by the new coming baby and this feeling may persist for years. It is best that the elder child be included in the preparation for the baby's arrival. He should be told what changes will take place with a newborn baby in the house. Parents should make special time for him after the baby is born, and listen to how he feels about the change. He should also be allowed to participate in baby care by helping the baby get dressed or pushing the stroller.

Rachel's story highlights one other problem in a loveless family—that of a family star. The love-deficient environment sets the stage for a particular family member to assume the role of a star. The family star assumes that his own personal interests, pursuits and experiences are more interesting and significant than those of anyone else in the family. He takes for granted that he is entitled to the most attention and the most resources. He wants the other family members to stay in the background and be supporting players only. He believes that the family rules that apply to others do not necessarily apply to him. He may try to control everything about his sibling and insists that the latter has to ask permission to do things that he himself can do without asking. This is because he wants everyone to recognise that he is superior in status.

The star may say things that have little conviction behind them and get away with it. He treats others as if they are his puppets. He gets his sibling in trouble with their parents, regardless of how much the sibling will have to suffer. If the star is good at chess, his sibling cannot be very good at it. If he is a B student, the sibling cannot be an A student. He openly reads his sibling's secret diary and ridicules what the sibling has written. He divulges negative remarks that others have made about his sibling. He considers himself the authority on what constitutes a good movie, what books should be read and what emotions should be permitted at home. Anything that is unattractive in his eyes will have no place in his world. He assumes that his sibling cannot think of anything that he does not already know. The list goes on.

Making a Child Feel Loved
Beyond fulfilling their child's biological needs, parents must provide a safe and nurturing environment for his healthy growth. What is often missing is the lack of empathic listening on the parents' part. Simply listening to the child with the intent

to understand and refraining from imposing our point of view goes a long way in establishing rapport with the child. We can offer direction and guidance, but only after we have listened and understood him. For a child to be loved, he needs to feel that he has been heard, that he has shared and that other family members have listened.

It is not uncommon for parents to tell a child they have worked hard to get him into junior college and university and he must stop whining and get straight A's in all his subjects. This does not help because such a remark makes the child feel that nobody cares for him. Beware of the quiet child who obtains straight A's and obeys all the family rules in silence. He may be feeling unloved and harbour deep resentment which has distanced him from family love.

When a child opens up his feelings about his negative experiences, a frequent response from parents is to tell him that the child is always in the wrong no matter what happens. They may add on the derogatory remark, "How much do you understand about life at your age?" They think that such an approach would make the child grow into a stronger person and this has often to do with the parents not being able to see the child as an individual. The child is expected to conform to parental judgments regardless of the situation. In time, he would start doubting the wisdom and worthiness of adults and stop sharing his personal issues with his parents. He would end up with a tense inner life after deciding that nobody in his environment makes sense. Loneliness will teach him to avoid sharing his feelings. In the absence of help to change his unproductive life patterns he feels disenchanted and inadequate in dealing with this reality. It is important for the adult to recognise the child's need for help at this stage.

The most effective way to help a child feel loved is to advise him instead of instructing him. Guidance on his developmental path and coping methods should be provided instead of interventions to solve his problem for him. The child must be given a sense of direction so that he feels that he remains the source of his own achievement. Taking a step back to facilitate the child's development of independence without losing parental authority is the way to go.

During adolescence, parents should start to provide their wisdom to help the young person make his own decision. Familiarising the growing child with all the diverse ways of making a living and letting him choose his own career would be a recommended approach. If parents love their child, they should encourage and not possess him. They must love their kid when he succeeds and love him when he fails. They simply need to listen and be supportive.

Parents must help their child to acquire emotional well-being. Praise, encouragement and affectionate attention are the building blocks of healthy emotions and self-esteem. They must avoid sarcasm, neglect and bullying. Helping him to develop a positive self-perception and a sense of safety goes a long way in making him feel loved. Their need to impose their authority and take charge comes only when boundaries are transgressed. As parents, it is better that they play the role of givers rather than receivers.

Chapter 3

Low Self-Esteem and Depression

THE link between depression and low self-esteem has been established in many studies. Commonly, with low self-esteem the child tends to experience fluctuations in their emotions and perceive other people in his life as rejecting him. In general, too little self-esteem makes people feel defeated and lead them to make bad choices. It is as if they are driving through life with hand-brakes on their vehicles. They can fail to live up to their full potential or fall into destructive relationships.

The concept of self-esteem is closely connected with the idea of personal value. It is a complex combination of beliefs about the self that develops in early childhood and reflects a person's subjective emotional evaluation of his self-worth as he matures into adulthood. It involves his ability to handle life's challenges and to feel accepted and liked. It also paves the way for him to interact competently in his circle of friends, identify his values, live up to his life potential, give love to others and be loved.

Self-esteem is built on a foundation of trust, security and unconditional love in the early stages of one's life. As the child grows, positive evaluations will enhance his self-esteem whereas negative evaluations will destroy it. Likewise, self-esteem is enhanced when the child is able to make favourable comparisons with other people or with an ideal self when he is able to perform effectively in his social and physical environment.

A good opinion and respect for oneself generates a sense of well-being. This is largely determined by the person's previous successes, aspirations and family hopes on him. A lot depends on what he perceives as his value to the world and how valuable he thinks he is to other people. This lies at the core of his self-concept and affects his trust in others and his relationships.

Self-Concept

Our self-concept is the overall view of the unconscious belief we have of ourselves, our attributes, who we are and what the self is all about. The essence of self-concept is the sense of being distinct from other people and the awareness that one possesses unique qualities, including appearance, skills, temperament and attitudes. This view is heavily influenced by the way in which a person interprets the feedback he receives from other people and the way he perceives their reactions to what he does and says.

As a rule, most of us try to behave in a manner that fits in with our self-concept. The gap between one's perceived self and one's ideal self gives an indication of his self-esteem. If a person's view of himself is close to how he would like to be, then he can be said to have healthy self-esteem.

JENNY ON SELF-ESTEEM, SOCIAL COMPARISONS AND RELATIONSHIPS

Jenny, a thirty-year-old who has been suffering from chronic anxiety since her college days, shares with me how her concept of what she wanted to achieve academically pushed her into depression with multiple suicidal attempts. During the interview, Jenny gives an account of the extent to which she has been affected by her perception of how the world judged her. This happened even after getting into university and her anxiety worsened as she continued to make comparisons between herself and others.

I have attempted suicide twice before. Actually in secondary school I have already thought of jumping down and killing myself should I fail to score the points I wanted. In my second year of college, I didn't do well. Apart from cutting myself, I took an overdose of Panadol one day after my exam results came out. I took twenty tablets. It was embarrassing. How can I as a top student drop to the bottom few? But I didn't die, just bad stomach aches and persistent vomiting from the overdose.

My 'A' Level results were worse than what I expected. In subjects that I used to score either an A or a B, I got C's.

In university I did even worse. I kept cutting my wrist because of the pressure to score well. Also, there was pressure from my ex-boyfriend in university. He would compete with me for results, to see who scored higher. After every test we compared answers to find out who was right and who was wrong, and it was very stressful while we were waiting for results. He would keep analysing my performance to tell me why I couldn't score adequately for First Class Honours. He also had a violent and bad temper. I was so stressed that my hair kept dropping. Finally I got my First Class Honours and I felt better. I always carried a penknife in my bag and I would use it to cut myself whenever my boyfriend gave me stress.

After graduation I found a job as a research assistant. I didn't really like myself in work life. Despite physical abuse from my *boyfriend, I still stuck on with him because I wouldn't know how to be with any other guy. I stayed on with him simply because I needed a boyfriend. I just accepted him because I didn't have anyone else.*

I do not know how I acquired this mentality of feeling shameful about being single. I still have this feeling today. Last weekend at a wedding lunch, my ex-colleague asked me about my marital status and commented that if I still did not get married by 31, it would be too late because a girl's shelf life was short.

To me it is very embarrassing if I don't have a boyfriend. I couldn't stand my ex-boyfriend anymore. We broke off eventually and he got married to someone else. So, all those guys that I was with have all got married, while I am still single. I ask myself: "What's wrong with me?"

Developmental Perspectives

The quality of esteem development in the adolescent's early growth phase largely determines the extent to which he develops trust and warmth or become suspicious and hostile towards others in later life. From the moment a baby is born, self-esteem develops as part of his blossoming identity. Parents respond lovingly to his smiles and cries as he feels loved and cherished. At school age, the child relies a lot on his parents and teachers to affirm that he is being loved and approved of. A child whose early life experiences have been favourable to the building of healthy self-esteem is able to internalise the feelings of self-worth and gradually become less dependent on others for approval.

Otherwise, if he still has to rely on external sources for his self-esteem, he will find it tough to handle life challenges. A child with low self-esteem is prone to anxiety. He often says that he is unhappy, hates himself and concerned about how other people perceive him. On the other hand a child with high self-esteem speaks confidently of himself and with pride.

With adolescent growth, there is a transition from being dependent on parents to a state in which he starts to figure out how he fits into the greater scheme of his social environment. This is a period of uncertainty in his life and he is likely to face significant emotional and mental upheaval. The loss of his original identity may lead to a feeling of vulnerability. In the meanwhile, he struggles to rediscover who he is as an independent individual. During this period of development, he may want to conform to social expectations in order to receive the approval of his peers. Otherwise he may want to take on responsibilities and tasks in which he is likely to succeed so that he feels efficacious. Both approaches will help to enhance his self-esteem.

We all require some sense of belonging to a group. After all, this is a primal human need, just like the need for food, clothing and shelter. Belonging means being accepted as a member. There are some people who seek belonging through excluding others based on the reasoning that there must be people who don't belong in order for there to be those who do. Unfortunately, this approach works against esteem building. A single instance of a child being excluded from a sports team can undermine his self-confidence and well-being and create pain and conflict.

Our society and culture place great emphasis on evaluation

of individual merit and tend to be unforgiving of mistakes made. Children are graded in their academic performance and athletic achievements or co-curricular activities in schools. In turn, the schools are ranked according to their students' overall performance standards. Parents often compare their children's school achievements with those of other families as they try to keep up with the social standing of their friends and neighbours. Such social comparisons plant the seed for anxiety in the child. He will start asking: "How am I in comparison with my classmates? Which group membership will make my school life happier?" To him, peer acceptance is uncertain and his personal worth is not assured. He is mentally occupied with comparing himself with others and doubting his efficacy. Under such circumstances more questions surface. He wonders if he has found a place to which he can comfortably belong and if others will respect him in this new group. He will also question whether he has managed to accomplish what he should be doing.

Low esteem leads to anxiety and a distorted view of oneself and others. A characteristic of children with low self-esteem is their difficulty in forming close attachments. This is simply because they find it difficult to believe that they are worthy of a fulfilling relationship with someone else. They have difficulty setting goals and solving problems. They tend to deny their successes while placing little value on their own abilities. With a lowered level of self-confidence they fear failure of attaining their academic potential, expect the worst in life and are handicapped by self-limiting beliefs.

HAZEL ON EFFECTS OF LOW SELF-ESTEEM

Hazel shared with me her experience of growing up with low self-esteem and how it took a toll on her mental well-being.

I grew up with low self-esteem and the people around me made me feel like my presence was never significant. I felt like my feelings didn't matter and was taken for granted all the time. I remember I wanted to end my life when I was about 14 or 15 years old. I just couldn't stand being around people as I felt useless and unwanted.

As I grew older, the repressed feelings of uselessness would still linger more than it should, causing waves of anxiety, sleepless nights and much tears. With this negativity constantly at the back of my head, I short-changed my expectations. The yearning to have someone like me was profound, especially when I started dating.

I dated someone who was very emotionally abusive and yet I stayed with him for almost two years. Subsequently I had another relationship but it ended abruptly just because his mother didn't like me. He didn't tell me why at first despite my begging to know the reason. It was so painful when I got to know about it eventually because I felt it was very unfair that he just concluded that he didn't like me without even getting to know me. Subsequently I found out he had also been cheating on me. He made a girl pregnant and the discovery broke my heart. I couldn't focus on whatever I was doing and it took a toll on me. I lost so much weight and was so depressed that I had to see a counsellor because I really needed help. It took me more

*than two years to overcome my depression but I am blessed
that I am now emotionally stronger than I was before.*

Mood Influence

One way to understand the emotion behind self-esteem is to
understand the concept of mood. Many people feel that low
self-esteem has been a key contributor to their low mood and
depression to start with. Some of them have been bullied because
they are shy or reserved. In turn, experiencing depression wears
their self-confidence down further. Some also feel that depression
has changed the way they see themselves.

Like emotions, moods fluctuate over time. It is a mental
disposition that is elated at one extreme in which a person
is aroused and ready to act, and at the other extreme he feels
fearful, listless and anxious and is reluctant to take action. Mood
influences thoughts and actions but it is also influenced by the
events and experiences in the world of the maturing adolescent.
A positive mood encourages him to perceive the world in benign
terms and fosters the perception of a self at ease and accepted by
other people around him. It produces momentary positive self-
evaluation which creates certainty about his self-worth.

In contrast, a negative mood encourages him to perceive the
social world as hostile. He sees a self that is at risk living within
and this leads him to wonder about how others will respond to his
actions and his chances of success in his endeavours. He adopts
self-limiting beliefs because he sees obstacles with unfriendly
people in his life path and limited chances for achievement.

Mood is related to how successfully the person has attained

his goals in his social world. If a school child falls short of the expectations of his parents or teachers, he feels disappointed, ashamed and depressed. In the mental state of shame, the mood is influenced by the emphasis on the individual responsibility for his performance and outcome. Feeling that he has failed, he has now to endure the shame of facing a world of judging people before him.

On the other hand, a person who believes in himself and is self-reliant is more likely to be able to cope with his failure. He will be able to weather the occasional storm and regain his equilibrium more readily. With increased resilience he is more likely to enjoy life and form more successful, fulfilling relationships than someone with low self-esteem.

Foundations for Healthy Self-Esteem

It is of utmost importance to know the natural ground for building healthy self-esteem in our children. To start with, we will have to fully accept our child as he is. Guiding him into the educational and social world at his own pace and respecting his unique qualities is fundamental. He must understand how his character is different from those of other people.

Next, we need to listen to the child's feelings and refrain from criticising him as he struggles with his life problems. Instead, we should use realistic praise for the efforts he puts in and for his accomplishments. Allowing him to discover his way of coping with new situations and encouraging him to keep trying when he is challenged are important. Within the home it helps to delegate responsibilities to him that are appropriate for his age and skills.

The maturing adolescent needs the adult to shine light on his path towards independence. To this end it helps if we show interest in what captivates him in his schoolwork and make it explicit that we are proud of his uniqueness. Along the way, we need to spend time to teach him how to handle disappointments. There is much value in taking a walk with him together and listening to his account of his social experiences. Playing games with him or planning family outings together are also of help because we are showing him that we experience joy in being with him.

As parents, we need to be conscious of the fact that we are the child's most powerful mirror in which he can use to see his reflected self. Hence, we need to evaluate our own level of security and esteem and model to our child our capability of handling challenging situations. The child's earliest perceptions of himself stem from his internalisation of parent's attitudes. If the parent-child relationship is positive in the pre-school years, he experiences himself as a worthwhile, successful, and loved individual. As the child grows we will need to help him to develop a strong sense of self and understand how he fits into the social world around him. Doing so would require him to have a clear awareness of his personal values and guiding principles in life.

There will be times when the child's insecurities interfere with his ability to accept who he is and his social functioning. When this happens we need to address his issues head on. As parents, we may want to explore those areas of his life that shape his self-worth and self-confidence. Contrary to popular belief, self-esteem does not come by simply telling the child that he is wonderful and great. Instead, it comes from cumulative experiences that have made him feel capable, effective and accepted.

When the child learns to do things for himself and feels proud of what he can do, he starts feeling capable. So, we should help our child to develop an understanding of who he is and where he can fit into his own social environment. He may also need help to identify what he values in his life and what qualities he admires in others. If he admires someone who is kind, loving and charitable, he too may like to develop the same qualities in himself. We may then want to guide him into reflecting over what he needs to do to live in accordance with those values, and furthermore, how to use his personal values to build his guiding principles in life.

For instance, if a child values charity and kindness he may want to join a social group and participate in volunteer work. Along the way he may want to set goals that are in accordance with his values. The moment he realises how he can attain his set goals, he will feel capable and ready to embark on his journey of esteem building. He will also feel the effectiveness in himself when he sees that positive results are coming out of his efforts.

Next, we need to be aware that the child's self-esteem has a deep connection with parenting styles, a topic that is discussed in greater depth in the next chapter.

Let us take the example of the authoritarian style in which parents are strict and controlling. In this style, the family rules are clear but rigid and inflexible. The parents are aloof and unresponsive to the child's emotional needs. They do not allow room for the discussion of his problems. Bad behaviours in their eyes are punished. Hence children with authoritarian parents develop low self-esteem because they are not allowed to have choices, make decisions or express their opinions. While they may perform well in schoolwork, they tend to become followers rather than leaders. They have a hard time relating to peers and playing with others. In general, those children who have been abused verbally, emotionally, physically or traumatised in some way when they were young would tend to have difficulty in developing high self-worth and coping with life challenges.

It is useful therefore to help the child discover his strengths and weaknesses and accept the fact that making mistakes is a natural and effective way of learning. An important source of positive self-esteem comes from the drive for achievement and the joy of seeking, learning, creating and competing. Interactions with other people form the basis of self-concept and a solid self-concept is associated with self-mastery and effective coping abilities.

Keep in mind that the child's failure to conform to self-imposed standards of performance in the academic or sports arena can also injure his self-esteem. Do help him to learn what he is capable of and set realistic and challenging goals. If necessary, compile a list of all his strengths and post it on his bedroom wall to remind him of his qualities. Accumulate all his accomplishments such as trophies, awards and certificates and put them on a shelf and let him spend some time looking at his accomplishments regularly. At the same time it is crucial that you do not let him dwell on his weaknesses.

It is also important to help the child develop creativity in self-expression and recognise the unique ways in which he can express himself. Some children use artistic means such as drawing, painting, colouring and writing to provide an outlet for the strong emotions that they deal with. Others may prefer to express themselves through playful expression with interactive games, sports or through the building of objects like dollhouses or model cars.

How Parents Can Help

Impress on the child that he has the right to be himself and that he can make a difference to the world. Sometimes even the mere act of talking about earning self-esteem can motivate the child. Assist him to imagine a future self so that he can focus on attaining his goals. Help the child to learn how to take care of himself. While life can be difficult he has to be reminded that there are ways and things he can do to smoothen the path for himself. Teach him to ask himself each day what is he is grateful for. Even when things are going tough, so long as he can identify one thing each day for which he can be thankful, such as good weather, he can help himself to feel good.

It is often upsetting for parents to hear their child speaking about his suffering and hopelessness. One common reaction from parents is to point out the good things the child already has in life and remind him how fortunate he already is, and that he should be contented. This is a mistake. Such an approach makes him feel that he is not understood and discourages him from confiding in his parents thereafter. Rather, the parents should comment on what the child considers as his suffering in such a way that the child feels that there is interest in his well-being and

that the parent is making an effort to understand.

Whether or not a child appears to care, he needs plenty of encouragement from the parent. Simple words of praise and paying attention to the good things he does or says every day makes a big difference in his life. One example is to tell him that you notice that he is making a greater effort at schoolwork or he is playing the piano livelier than before. You may like to thank the child for helping to clear the table and wash the cutlery after dinner. Commenting on any small signs of progress in his daily life is a good way to help him get back on track.

Spending enjoyable and relaxed time with a teenager is often helpful when he is depressed. This can be difficult because the depressed child may be caught up with his own life and want to remain alone. However it is a worthwhile effort to think of creative ways to spend one-on-one time with the child. Shopping together in a mall or watching a movie together can help. Remember that it is often the informal time spent together that is more valuable. A good time to chat is when you are picking him up in a car from school.

Sometimes parents are worried that listening to the teenager's upsets will encourage him to get more stuck in his negative thoughts and push him further towards suicidal tendencies. The truth is that the child needs the parent not only to listen and accept their concerns but also to reassure him that help is available should he need somebody to cheer him up. It is when a child is allowed or left to ruminate over his sufferings and blame himself for his difficulties will he tend to spiral down into depression.

Let us not forget that it is emotionally exhausting to handle anxious children. Concerned parents feels that they cannot leave their depressed children alone. They need to remember to recharge their own batteries, such as regular exercise, spending time with their own social circle or even joining a support group for people with depressed family members. Caring for one depressed child puts strain on the whole family and the other children may feel overlooked and start to resent. As a parent you need to explain to them your perspective of the depressed child's difficulties. Giving time to the other children may help them to understand and cope better with the situation. Do not abandon your family holidays because the depressed child may also want to participate and enjoy a break. All families have problems. A healthy family would acknowledge the existence of a problem, discuss them together and take steps to solve them.

Chapter 4

Parenting and Attachment Styles

IF children are to thrive emotionally, they need a close, continuous attachment relationship with their parents or caregivers who are available both physically and psychologically. Attachment is an emotional bond that ties one person with another. This bond would involve a desire for one to be in regular contact with another person to the extent that a feeling of distress would be evoked if he is separated from that person.

The characteristic feature of attachment behaviour is the intensity of the emotion that accompanies the process. Parenting can therefore be approached from this viewpoint. If all goes well with the child-parent relationship, there is joy and a sense of security. Otherwise the young person would feel threatened, anxious and angry. If the attachment is broken, there will be grief and a tendency to depression.

Emotional Bonds

Children are born with an innate drive to form attachments with parents and caregivers. The earliest bonds have a significant impact on their later life development. Different attachment behaviours in the infant serve different functions. By smiling and cooing, the child alerts the parent or caregiver that he desires interaction. By crying and kicking, he triggers a quick response from the adult to provide problem-solving or protection and safety. When he feels distressed with a need to get into close proximity with the secure base, the child displays the active behaviour of reaching for or clinging to his parent or caregiver.

Barely a generation or two ago, many adults lived with the paradigm that too much love and affection by a parent or caring for one's child sensitively would make him a spoilt brat. It used to be a widespread belief then that something was wrong with mothers who coddled their children or were too involved with their upbringing. Too much of closeness has been labelled as harmful for child growth and maturation. With improved understanding of attachment behaviour[5] we now know that the mother-child attachment is instrumental in shaping the child's mental development and self-esteem. In turn, the child's self-esteem shapes his ability to attract and maintain successful relationships as he matures into adulthood. Anxiety builds up whenever physical separation or a loss of the attachment figure occurs. In the event that a child is subjected to a prolonged or repeated separation from parents, he is exposed to prolonged unresolved distress and this situation sows the seed for anxiety and depression in later life.

The special bond between the infant and the parent is by no means unique to the human species. Such a desire for the presence of the parent is observed throughout the animal kingdom and is part of an evolutionary ability for living beings to adapt to the natural world. During World War II, psychiatrists had observed that infants in hospitals and orphanages who were separated from their parents suffered from impaired social and psychological development. We have since realised that the parent-child relationship provides the key experience that connects the personal and social worlds of the child. It is the dynamic interplay between these two worlds that allows the child's social competence to evolve. Increasingly, it is recognised that there is a strong link between insecure attachments and depressive symptoms in the child's maturation journey.

---

5   The theory of attachment was originally developed by Dr. John Bowlby (1907-1990) a psychoanalyst who was working towards understanding the nature of the distress of infants who were separated from their parents. By the 1980s it was increasingly realised that attachment processes also play out in adulthood.

Parent-Child Attachment

In his earliest experience, the infant has a desire to be near his mother because this keeps him secure and provides him with a safe haven. The secure base allows the child to explore the world while knowing that he can always return to the safety of the mother when needed. For most children, the primary attachment figure is usually the mother, but they may also have a more limited attachment relationship with other people, including the father, grandparents and older siblings. The role of the primary caregiver must be stable for at least the first three to five years, the period when a child's brain develops most rapidly.

The main benefit of attachment to the child is protection from danger. The behaviour and emotions associated with attachment are most clearly seen in situations of anxiety and distress, including those involving fear, danger and conflict and uncertainty about the caregiver's availability.

By the end of the first year, the child's attachment behaviour becomes activated when there are frightening circumstances during which the mother was inaccessible. Commonly, the child becomes upset when parents leave him in the care of others

whereas the sound and reappearance of the mother would often terminate the behaviour. In more intense situations, the child would cling on to the mother for added security. In very intense situations, the child may even need a prolonged cuddle.

Typically, there are three attachment styles in children: secure, anxious-ambivalent and avoidant-insecure. Infants who are securely-attached use their parents as a secure base while they explore their surrounding environment. These infants are able to separate from the parents without distress and feel happy when the parents come back. Whenever they are scared, they seek comfort from their parents or caregivers. The parents react quickly to their needs and the children are certain that their parents will be responsive.

Infants who belong to the anxious-ambivalent group have difficulty using the parent or caregiver as a secure base. When the child is separated from the parent he is often highly distressed but is generally ambivalent when the parent returns. He is reluctant to explore his environment and is wary of strangers even when the parent is present. This is a result of poor maternal availability.

In contrast, those infants who belong to the avoidant-insecure attachment group do not exhibit distress when the parent departs nor display much emotion when the parent returns. They tend not to explore much and tend to avoid parents or caregivers. When offered a choice they show no preference between a caregiver and a stranger. This attachment style may be the result of neglect.

Children who are securely attached as infants tend to develop positive self-esteem, a stronger self-identity and self-reliance as they mature. They also tend have less anxiety and depression, be more independent and have healthy social relationships. In turn, relationships that are developmentally healthy would allow the individual to see himself as a secure and autonomous being who is willing to accept and seek help.

Parents and caregivers need to understand what children need from other people in order to develop into healthy adults, and what happens when these needs are not met. Many depressed children have child-parent relationships that are characterised by neglect, confusion, hurt and abuse. What the child recalls are typically memories or scenes of indifference, rejection and disappointment.

Parent-child relationships are not the only determinants of a child's behaviour, but knowledge of his past socio-emotional experiences may provide us with an insight into his personality and the character of his interpersonal life. The relationship between the early experiences of parental care, growth and behaviour are complexly determined, but attachment experiences are one important element in the big picture. We may find the interplay between the child's past and present experiences, and between his inner psychological self and outer social self are both complex and daunting. However, we do know that certain parenting styles and family relationship patterns promote aggressive and poorly adjusted children.

An important point to note is that when attachment behaviour is high, exploratory behaviour is low. In a situation where a child experiences a high anxiety level all the time, he will have less time and energy to enjoy the benefits of exploration, enquiry and natural curiosity. This suppression of exploratory behaviour is likely to adversely affect the development of adaptive and survival skills in his psychosocial environment.

Attachment in Infants, Toddlers and School Children

Human infants are born with a natural tendency to develop in a socially cooperative way. Characteristically from the moment of birth, the parents' attention is focused on the baby because something unique about the infant draws every family member to the new arrival. The sensitive mother quickly tunes in to her infant's natural feeding and sleeping rhythms and discovers what suits the baby and how best to respond accordingly. This process makes the baby contented and cooperative. The desire to maintain close proximity to one's parents during early infancy is usually so strong that in the event the child is suddenly separated from his parents for a period of time, he will become distressed, and refuse to be consoled or looked after by anyone else. Usually it is the mother with whom the infant establishes the greatest attachment. However, the infant will form an attachment with any person who takes the mother's role at an early age.

Attachment behaviour brings infants into close proximity with their caregivers and it is through this close relationship that children learn about themselves, other people, the nature of behaviour and social life. Through understanding the display of emotions, the child begins to take note of other people's affective states. As the child begins to talk and becomes more mobile during the second and third years of life, parents usually attempt to shape the child's social behaviour by teaching him new skills. Adding guidance on to the affection prepares the child better in interacting with other members of his social group.

By the time the infant reaches toddler stage, there is less need for him to be in physical proximity to the parents. Instead, he has a greater need to be independent. He begins to separate and function with increasing autonomy. Just knowing that his parents are psychologically available will suffice in bringing feelings of security.

Within close relationships, young children acquire mental models of their own worthiness based on other people's availability and willingness to provide care and protection. This ability to model one's environment increases understanding and effectiveness and helps in achieving social competence. It is from his relationship with other people that he learns to understand himself, and through that, understand other people. So his world of relationships is the means to the solution he seeks. However, this also means that the quality of these close relationships has a profound impact on how the self, others and social interaction are understood by him. The child develops ideas and expectations and beliefs about how the self is viewed and understood and the way that other people respond in times of distress and anxiety. These expectations and beliefs are built up over the first months and years of life and the psychological models lay down the trajectory for the child's subsequent development.

As the child's attachment relationships are internalised, the quality of the child's social experiences becomes a mental property. It influences his view of himself and others, affects behaviour, relationship style and social competence, and gradually shapes his personality.

As growth continues, the child develops an increasing tolerance for separation from his parents. He feels more at ease to play in their absence. By school age, he can be separated from parents for many hours without signs of distress. This is a reflection of the child's growing desire to explore the world around him. He soon learns that being out of their parents' presence does not mean he has been abandoned. This enables him to play outside and away from home as he grows older. As confidence in the child-parent relationship increases, he starts to develop alternative attachment relationship with his own special group of friends.

Attachment in school children is a product of felt security resulting from the availability of protection within a child-teacher relationship. Safe-haven behaviour may be manifested even within a relationship that does not have enduring emotional ties. For instance a school kid may feel safer to explore the academic challenges in school because his favourite teacher is around, even though she may not be his attachment figure.

By middle childhood, the child is increasingly able to reason out things for himself and adapt goals for his activities. He begins to prioritise his actions in the interest of a bigger plan and acquires new information for problem solving. Being better able to understand his own point of view as well as that of his caregiver, he can regulate and communicate his emotions better. He becomes more sophisticated in his planning and better able to execute them.

Latch-Key Kids

There is a special situation when a child becomes more prone to anxiety and depression — that of a latch-key kid. Some families do not have the financial means to send their children to supervised care after school. So when a latch-key child comes home to an empty house, he lacks adequate adult supervision and is left to care for himself most of the time. Latch-key kids may have a higher incidence of insecure attachment. These children are characterised by a fear in self-care and this lowers the child's self-esteem and influences his social adjustment. These children are generally more anxious because of the lack of adult protection and security after school. Being home alone to care for oneself is itself a frightening experience. In the absence of adequate attention from parents or coping strategies, the child lacks the tools to mature properly. This can potentially affect his sense of self and his ability to adapt to new and different situations.

CLEMENT ON ABSENT PARENTS AND ANXIETY

Clement has just turned forty and been confronting the impact of depression on his life and career change. He is bitter over his childhood in a loveless family environment and recalls how his experience of being a latch-key kid had a significant contribution to his depression.

There wasn't much interaction between my father and I as a kid. Except for schoolwork and household matters where he would coach as a teacher, we didn't sit down and chat. He preferred to keep to himself. When he came home from school in the late evening, he'd sit in the back room until dinner was ready. After dinner, he'd be in the same room by himself.

There wasn't much physical closeness either. This was a family that didn't touch much – no hugs, no pats and no strokes. Until today, I occasionally feel awkward giving someone a hug.

As both my parents were teachers, we were always in the care of baby-sitters after school hours. I was about nine or ten then. The latch-key situation came about when my father (presumably) fell-out with the family of our next-door neighbour; their mother was our after-school baby-sitter/nanny.

That period was also the period of the breakdown of my parents' already strained marriage. Apparently, it had been simmering since I was born, according to my father. Instead of arranging for another after-school care, my father felt I was old enough to hold keys. Safekeeping the keys to our house gave me a lot of anxiety. Besides incurring my father's wrath should I lose them, we were brought up with his constant frightening messages that the neighbourhood was not safe. All doors had to be locked and double-checked.

Being at home alone can be a frightening and dangerous experience for children. Parents can help the latch-key child by going through the home routines with him. They can also train the child to take precautions such as instructing him to tell callers that their parents are "busy" instead of indicating that he is alone at home. They may want to arrange for the child to spend some afternoons with friends to break the monotony. Children can be taught that independence and resourcefulness are virtues, but they must not be given too many responsibilities. They must also be allowed to voice their fears. It is a good idea for the parents to establish goodwill with neighbours and ask if they are willing to step in if their child needs help. In the meanwhile they will continue to need family support in terms of emergency telephone numbers, communication between siblings and listening to their input with regards to family matters.

Making sense of his past childhood has been not easy for Clement. We know that kids who are left unsupervised for long periods of time tend to feel abandoned, frustrated, angry and sometimes in despair. Being left alone and in a family in disarray are probably the main determinants of his depression. Researchers have found that, for an elementary school child, anything more than 12 hours a week of being left alone is harmful and predisposes them to depression. Significant other adults need to be in the child's life if parents are absent for long periods of time. There should also be ways for the child to fill the hours instead of being loaded with adult responsibilities and left to fend for himself.

Generally speaking, the effects of being a latch-key kid differ with age. For children below ten, fear, loneliness and boredom are the most common. In the early teens they tend to be more susceptible to peer pressure such as alcohol and drug abuse. As they grow older, they are more likely to show behavioural problems and exhibit a higher risk of clinical depression with low self-esteem as compared with other children. However, under the right family circumstances, a latch-key kid can benefit from early acceptance of self-care responsibilities. What is needed is for the parents to maintain ongoing or supportive communication with him, and be sensitive to his behavioural and emotional changes. He also needs to be openly praised for meeting his self-care responsibilities.

Attachment in Adolescents and Adults

Adolescence is a transition period in which the individual is making a tremendous effort to be less dependent on attachment figures. Despite this, the attachment behaviour is not relinquished but gradually transferred to peers. This transforms the attachment relationships from a situation in which he primarily receives care from others to a peer attachment relationship in which he both receives and offers care. In a cross-gender situation, one of the endpoints of this relationship is the development of romance which eventually becomes a lifelong attachment.

The growing adolescent often appears as if he is actively and purposefully running away from his attachment relationship with parents. The bond with parents is treated more like a tie that restrains him rather than an anchor that provides security. In fact, a key task of the adolescent's development of autonomy is to eliminate the need to rely on parental support when making his way into society.

The period of adolescence is characterised by a dramatic increase in differentiation of the self from others. This differentiation allows for a more consistent view of the self as existing apart from interaction with parents. At this stage, he may realise that parents may be deficient in some ways in meeting his attachment needs while other relationships may meet his attachment needs better. He may then move on with greater openness, flexibility and objectivity in evaluating past relationships. This is characteristic of a secure attachment in adolescence.

As the adolescent grows he becomes more sophisticated in managing his attachment relationship with his parents in terms of set goals. If he wants to stay out past midnight he may take into consideration not only his own desire to stay out late, but also the goal in maintaining trust and warmth with his parents. This decreased reliance on parents as attachment figures needs to be understood by parents in the correct context. The change reflects a decrease in dependence rather than a lowered importance of the relationship.

The ability to function with greater social and emotional autonomy is a critical developmental milestone. This autonomy does not necessarily develop in isolation but also in the context of a close enduring relationship with parents. A careful balance between attaining autonomy and maintaining relatedness with parents is the key to achieving attachment security. The autonomy-seeking behaviour can be considered part of an exploratory system, in which the adolescent seeks to live without being emotionally dependent on his parents. Without such exploration, social development such as establishing long-term romantic relationships and productive careers may be more difficult.

By mid-adolescence, interaction with peers takes on functions that provide important sources of intimacy, feedback about social behaviour, social influence, attachment relationships and lifelong partnerships. By late adolescence, the growing push for autonomy from parents leads to peers being used as attachment figures. With the development of peer relationships, romance tends to develop. The sexual and attachment drives both push the individual toward the development of new peer relationships with shared interests and strong affect. These eventually replace the functions of earlier child-parent relationships.

In adulthood, the attachment feelings are typically directed towards someone with whom adult life can be shared. There is a lot of similarity between these adult attachments with those of the parent-child relationship. Similar to infants, when adults experience consistent comfort from a relationship partner, they tend to be able to develop a sense of trust in other people and become more willing to disclose personal issues. This encourages them to seek out close relationships with others in stressful conditions and provides security. Likewise, unsatisfactory interactions with others produce insecurity. Those high in attachment anxiety are the ones who have received inconsistent support and caregiving in their past relationships. In addition, those who downplay their need for emotional bonds have probably experienced a lack of responsiveness from their partners.

Insecure Attachment Strategies

Two insecure attachment strategies, the *preoccupied* and *dismissive* strategies have been implicated in problems of psychosocial functioning.

It is common to encounter adolescent depression in association with parental attachment insecurity. The individuals tend to use a *preoccupied* strategy that is linked to internalising their problems and depression. Because their early attachment needs are not satisfied, they crave intimacy but feel doubtful about their own worth. They are often viewed as clingy and tend to seek extreme closeness to their partners to get emotional reassurance, while holding an irrational fear of being abandoned.

A depressed young lady once shared with me how she grew up with insecure attachment in a family with an absent father who worked as a seaman and came home only once in two years. Now, as a young working adult, she is emotionally affected whenever she is alone and has no friends to spend leisure time with. Recently, over one long weekend, she was so desperate at the thought of having to spend the weekend alone that she downloaded a friend-making app on her mobile phone and managed to make a new friend. She immediately went on a date with him only to find that the guy's interest was more in sex rather than in friendship.

People using a *dismissive* strategy are mainly concerned with maintaining autonomy and control in their relationships. They have a subconscious fear that caregivers are not reliable and intimacy is a dangerous thing. This often results in emotional distancing. People with a dismissive strategy are usually comfortable living independently and do not seek or desire close relationships. Self-sufficiency is a common trait.

I remember encountering an example of a dismissive strategy many years ago, when I was a young doctor working in the

A&E department of a public hospital. One evening a young man in his early twenties came to seek medical attention for his sprained wrist. The injury was mild but I arranged for an x-ray nonetheless. While explaining to him the features of the bony structures on the x-ray picture, I noticed that he suddenly turned emotional without any obvious reason. He recovered very quickly and remained composed. After some gentle probing, he divulged the fact that he was once a medical student but had given up his course of study halfway because of a relationship problem with his parents. Since then he has found a job, been attending evening classes in Accountancy and decided to stay completely away from home. He assured me confidently that he was moving on in his life very well, all by himself.

Parenting Styles

The child's development is deeply connected with two important dimensions of the parent-child relationship — how *responsive*

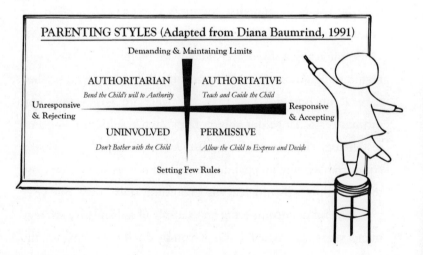

PARENTING STYLES (Adapted from Diana Baumrind, 1991)

Demanding & Maintaining Limits

AUTHORITARIAN
Bend the Child's will to Authority

AUTHORITATIVE
Teach and Guide the Child

Unresponsive & Rejecting

Responsive & Accepting

UNINVOLVED
Don't Bother with the Child

PERMISSIVE
Allow the Child to Express and Decide

Setting Few Rules

and how *demanding* the parents are. Responsive parents are warm and accepting toward their children, enjoy their company and are able to see things from their perspective. In contrast, non-responsive parents are aloof, rejecting, critical and insensitive to the child's emotional needs.

Parents who are demanding are firm on maintaining consistent standards for their child's behaviour. At the opposite end are lenient parents who provide little guidance and yield too often to their child's demands. Children are noted to develop better when the parents are both responsive and moderately demanding. Understanding the mix of responsiveness and demandingness allows four types of parenting styles to be identified and described.

Authoritative parents are both responsive and demanding and they discipline their child with love and affection. They tend to explain their rules and expectations to the child instead of simply forcing the rules on him. Children brought up with this parenting style tend to be self-reliant, self-controlled, cheerful and curious about new situations and skilled at play.

Authoritarian parents are not the same as authoritative parents. While they are also highly demanding, they differ in their style in that they demand blind obedience from their children instead of providing them with adequate knowledge of the situation, the options available and consequences of each option. They rely on strict discipline and want things their way, using enforcing statements such as "I want you to do this in this way because I say so." They frequently use physical punishment and withdrawal of affection to control and shape the child's behaviour. They are unresponsive to their children's needs and are generally not nurturing. Children who are treated this way tend to be moody, unhappy, fearful, irritable and socially withdrawn.

CLEMENT ON AUTHORITARIAN PARENTING AND ANXIETY

Clement, who earlier shared his experience as a latch-key kid, grew up in a family in which the father was an overly strict disciplinarian who used physical punishment. Shortly after his father's death, he began to reveal signs of depression and experience suicidal thoughts. He shares his views on how authoritarian parenting influenced his emotional state as a child.

I grew up in a home where my father was an authoritarian. Everything had to be done his way and according to his rigid rules. He'd get upset when those are not followed, including trivial rules like insisting that certain items must be stored in certain places only. For more severe matters, punishment was executed by caning our palms using the sawed-off end of a household feather duster.

My childhood anxiety stemmed from my father being the towering disciplinarian and wife-beater. I can't remember specifically what offences I was caned for, but the searing sensation was painful to the bone. While I remember myself as a rule-abiding and non-rebellious boy, I still ended up not following some of my father's rules and getting punished for it. His loud booming voice when he was scolding us also made me meek in front of him.

My father as the wife-beater probably cast a much scarier image of him than the image of myself being caned. I remember he took a wooden stool from the kitchen and kept swinging it at my mother who was cowered in a corner in a bedroom, with her hands blocking the blows. I could not fathom what would happen if he were to release that fury on my brother and me. Memories of the several occasions when he unleashed his fury on my mother still make my stomach churn today.

Permissive or indulgent parents are responsive, but are not demanding. They have few expectations of the children and impose little discipline. For example, if a kindergarten child is hungry and wants an additional snack, the parent will allow him to eat anything and everything he wants. Children treated in this manner tend to be low in both social responsibility and independence, but they tend to be more cheerful than the irritable children of the authoritarian parents.

Uninvolved parents are neither responsive nor demanding. They do not set firm boundaries or high standards for their children. They are generally neglectful or indifferent to the child's needs for affection and discipline and uninvolved in their lives. In contrast to the permissive parent in the above example, an uninvolved parent will not even respond to the child's hunger. Children who grew up under such parents tend to have impulsive behaviour, delinquency and even addiction. In the absence of self-regulation, they have a higher risk of encountering psychological difficulties and experiencing suicidal behaviour as they grow up.

Parenting Children with Attachment Issues

In contrast to children whose arrival to the world is met with kindness, children who have been neglected or abandoned often struggle with basic family life concepts. Many of them, who have been maltreated or abandoned in their early life, hold on to an erroneous belief that they are bad, defective or intrinsically deficient. This is especially pertinent in situations of child adoption. They may unconsciously believe that since he is basically defective, any improvement of behaviour is pointless. If this belief is not addressed, few parenting strategies will be of help.

Many parents who adopt children are unaware of the trauma or neglect that may have occurred during the child's infancy. They may be anticipating the adoption with excitement but when they realise that the beautiful child they love is not equipped to love them back in the manner they have hoped, it can be perplexing and disappointing. Attachment issues in children don't just disappear with adoption. These children struggle fundamentally with connection and relationship issues. However, with the right support they can experience significant healing and be better able to connect with others.

Providing the much needed attachment can help a troubled child to change his faulty beliefs. It is a good idea to strengthen the parent-child relationship through storytelling rather than just addressing his behavioural issues. For instance, parents can tell their child stories that model ways to handle different situations. Parents can also role play interactions using toys to illustrate a problem and possible solutions. With the growth of the parent-child attachment, many of the behavioural problems are likely to disappear because the child begins to change his self-view and understand that his parent or caregiver sincerely wants good things for him.

Apart from being provided with a healthy attachment, the child needs to have boundaries and discipline to learn how to navigate his life. He is likely to have acquired perceptual problems that parents or caregivers need to be aware of. The child is inclined to misinterpret other people's words and actions and place negative interpretations on them. Instead of seeking help when upset, he tends to feel comfortable with negative attention because that is in alignment with his past negative experiences and faulty belief system. He is frequently overwhelmed with strong internal emotions that obstruct his coping ability. Owing to his past experience with absent caregivers, he may have been taking care of himself without relying and others and have formed a strong controlling behaviour.

Because of the emotional immaturity and uneven or delayed development in children with attachment difficulties, there is seldom a single parenting technique that will work well for all ages. Apart from providing a more secure relationship, the parents or caregiver need to give the child a sense of self-mastery that would reverse his faulty belief and lead him into positive self-esteem. Helping the growing adolescent establish his identity as a human being with strengths and talents and with people around who love him is important.

A child who has been abandoned or neglected in the past tends to be more anxious and more easily overwhelmed by negative emotions and environmental noise or crowdedness. So the adult may need to calm the child down with special techniques before his behavioural problem can be addressed. The parents or caregiver must tailor their interventions to the child's unique needs and gauge their expectations according to the child's emotional age rather than his chronological age. If they expect him to act his chronological age, the child may become overwhelmed and in turn exhibit oppositional behaviour. What does not work at one stage may work later on. As a child becomes more attached to the caregiver and revises his core beliefs, it may become easier to convince the child that he does deserve good things in his life after all.

Despite the pain and difficulty that many parents have experienced with their child, their love usually turns out to be the most powerful source they have in the therapeutic process.

Chapter 5

Understanding Emotional Pain and Suicide

IT used to be a popular belief that no sane person would want to end his life, and those who want to end their life are assumed to be mentally ill and not just being miserable. With this orthodox view, suicide is construed as a product of psychological disturbance and the self-harmer is considered to be incapable of rational thought. The suicidal tendency is therefore perceived as an illness that drives an individual to kill himself. It is understandable, therefore, why our healthcare services feel a public responsibility to intervene and to prevent self-destructive behaviour. This perspective is further reinforced by the view that suicidal behaviour is a result of maladaptive attitudes grounded in mental illness.

Today, we are more inclined to dissent from this view. We are beginning to see the suicidal tendency as more of an indicator of emotional distress and despair. Rather than ascribing depressive illness as the underlying cause of suicide, we begin to see the individual as someone in chronic emotional pain who is struggling with misery and despair. With no hope of improvement in sight, he feels that he might as well be dead. If life circumstances are so distressful or painful, then death may well be an escape route for him. In fact, it is not uncommon for a young depressed child to harbour fantasies of suicide thinking that, if and when he is dead, his parents will regret their loss and will love him more. There is a danger however, that this fantasy may be further carried to the point of actual suicide when he reaches adolescence.

It is increasingly recognised that much of the emotional pain arising from an individual's anxiety has its origin in a lack of dialogue in early childhood. This is often compounded by a lack of a loving relationship, and  sometimes by grief over the loss of loved ones. Unfortunately, children are often taught and encouraged to contain their emotions by either isolating themselves or putting on a façade. Parents frequently send them out of the room when they start crying and expect them to settle down before they return. Harsher parents may introduce hurtful statements during those emotionally labile moments such as, "If you carry on crying, I shall give you more things to cry about." Adding irritation onto a child who is already being hurt is detrimental to his emotional growth. If he is unable to find love in his parents or caregivers, his immediate reaction would be to turn inwards to find solace. This will encourage his symptoms of mental upset to be buried even deeper.

The continual build-up of hurt in the child will eventually result in stress, misery and depression in later life. How this irritation will manifest is influenced by how the person copes. Many teenagers try to manage their accumulated stress and pain by resorting to cigarettes, alcohol, medication and self-destructive behaviour. The latter serves as a tool for providing temporary relief for an individual who has turned distress inwards on himself. If stress continues to infuse the individual to the extent that it is no longer possible for him to contain the pain in the depths of silenced fear, cries for help will begin to emerge.

When Despair Speaks from Within
During the adolescent growth phase, depression is usually present at some time or other. Anger and aggression often coexist but may remain buried. The ability to express anger may be temporarily stifled and directed inwards, giving the impression of meekness in the person. The child may have frequent panic attacks, crying spells and attacks of abdominal cramps with no obvious reason. He may lock himself up in a room or a toilet when he experiences panic attacks, and may become increasingly reluctant to go to school. Often, he has guilt feelings that are

difficult to tolerate, and in the absence of a sympathetic listener, he may be swamped by hopelessness and unworthiness. This may eventually lead to attempted self-destruction of the body in some way. However, the development of a self-harming habit in itself may not necessarily constitute a sufficient reason for the child to seek help.

Beware the adolescent who is avoiding social contacts or any other activities with his peers. He may be the object of bullying in school, or, he may be expressing something that is potentially dangerous. If he has given up his struggle and is completely unconcerned about his appearance, he may be sending a signal that he has lost hope and the ability to care.

Adolescent depression can be in the form of a persistently low mood when the sadness is never ending. It is disruptive to every part of the child's life, and provides fertile soil for suicidal thoughts to germinate. Not only does the adolescent feel hopeless, helpless and worthless, but the state of his mind also interferes with his schoolwork and peer relationships. Most adolescents would express the sentiment that a dysfunctional family is a major cause of their depression. Parents who are quarrelling and fighting at home or going through a separation or divorce, are a major contributor to childhood depression.

Parents and teachers are in the best position to recognise the signs of depression in adolescents. Being the people who are constantly in touch with them and their changes in moods and behaviour, they would know them better than mental health professionals. When in doubt, parents should trust their instincts.

Origin of Suicidal Thoughts

Suicidal thoughts in adolescence are more common than is generally envisaged. They may occur in response to a row, a broken relationship or a school exam failure. Often, warning signs exist. Whenever a child talks about death or suicide we must take it seriously. Likewise, changes in mood and behaviour that prevent the child from getting on in life should alert the parent or teacher that the child may have a depressive disorder. When in doubt, parents should trust their instincts. After all, parents know their child better than anyone else.

Many an adolescent suicide attempt follows a row with parents during which time he is suffused with anger and hate. His love and concern for himself and his parents are pushed aside as he sees his parents as being guilty of pushing him on to the verge of despair. The feeling of loss of control and helplessness gives him the idea that suicide may reverse the desperateness of the situation by helping him to regain his power over his own life. The notion of suicide nurtures the child's fantasy that his parents can be made to feel impotent and helpless while he is triumphant over the situation.

Many an adolescent who has attempted suicide on himself feels as if there is no choice but to do something that will silence the person who is mentally tormenting him. He feels pushed in the direction of his own death by a force which he may not understand at that moment. Sometimes the situation is more complex, especially when the adolescent tries to shield himself from the reality of death. There is a part of him that may want to kill himself while another part of him may want believe that something of himself will stay alive. He may end up putting himself to sleep with an overdose of medication without the intention of killing himself.

 ## CLEMENT ON EMOTIONAL PAIN AND DESPAIR

Clement, while struggling with his depression during his midlife crisis, recalls how parental disharmony at home was devastating to his childhood development.

A vivid memory was of a time when I was woken up in the middle of the night by my parents' loud quarrelling. This was when my father was out late, and my feisty mother suspected him of spending time with other women. She would ride the motorbike to track him down in a little town in Malaysia. Apparently, if she managed to find him, she would create a scene. They would then return home and quarrel.

I remember crying in bed and wanting the shouting to stop. Somehow the thoughts led me to the conclusion that it would be better if I were dead and out of the picture. They would then regret fighting so much and causing my death.

I was nine then. There was the memory of my father swinging a wooden stool at my mother and that reminded me of how frozen I was. I felt helpless at not being able to speak up about the violence, or to physically intervene during the attacks. These thoughts stopped when I was twelve and when my parents patched up. After that, I left for Singapore to study.

Many young people also try to kill themselves immediately after a devastating disappointment such as the breakup of a romantic relationship, the failure in an exam or the death of a parent. However, these are often preceded by other mental creations that have left him with the feeling that there is no alternative but to destroy his own body.

A normal, healthy adolescent knows he has ways of feeling valued and admired without having to be dependent on parents. Even when he has worrisome thoughts, he knows that these thoughts will not ultimately overwhelm him. However much despair or hopelessness he feels, he can rely on admiration from his own consciousness to restore self-respect. He possesses sufficient inner love to enable him to look forward to a future that can make amends for his own disappointments. He also has the inner freedom to forgive his parents who have let him down.

However, those adolescents who have gone through trauma and torment in their earlier childhood may experience things differently. Having suffered so intensely, they may not have ways of restoring their self-respect or undoing the harm their hurt feelings have caused them. The creations of their minds continue to haunt them. Some convince themselves that they have a mental pathology while others may believe that other people hate them. When he feels compelled to address what he believes is the source of pain or shame within him, things may become more serious. He may feel that the abnormal thoughts are lurking somewhere inside his self, and by giving in to the torment of the inner persecutor through suicide, he will experience relief.

CLEMENT ON SUICIDAL THOUGHTS IN THE TEENAGE YEARS

In my interview with Clement about his suicidal thoughts, he has identified four main factors that have contributed to his mental state. Of these factors, a loveless environment stands out clearly.

Firstly, I did not feel loved. We were a nuclear family, just my parents and us two kids. My father had severed ties with the rest of his siblings. On the random occasion when his siblings paid us a visit, he would refuse to open the door for them and wait in the back room until they left. I thought: Since I'm not loved by my father, why does it matter whether I'm alive or not? I won't be missed.

Secondly, there was much fear in my life. I lived in trepidation of my father's wrath, especially if I did something that went against his ways or rules. Although I was a filial son, I would occasionally do something wrong and get caned on the palm. I've never thought of running away though. I suspect that besides not knowing where to go, I was also fearful of my father's reaction. To me, fear of him represented a threat to my life, and ending my life would put an end to that threat.

Thirdly, I was sad about the state of my family life. My parents were regularly and heatedly quarrelling about their relationship at one stage in my childhood. I used to be gloomy about my family's fragile condition, though I was not preoccupied by it throughout the day. My mum moved out when I was 11, to avoid further beatings. In order to see my brother and me, she would visit us during school hours. I was not sure what my classmates or teachers thought, but they never asked.

Fourthly, rumination and scepticism reinforced my thoughts. I thought too much, even as a kid. My line of thought regularly concluded at the meaningless nature of life. The logical side concluded that since life is miserable, why prolong it?

Stigma and Shame of Suicide

Culturally, we saddle suicide with stigma. Stigma comes from the social message sent out that there is something fundamentally defective about the person who is suicidal. The stigma reinforces the idea that the suicidal person is bad, and that feeds into his shame. Committing suicide is likened to "self-murder" and the criminal language inherent in the lexicon heightens the stigma. In some legal systems, attempting suicide is considered a crime that is punishable by law. To this day, attempters of suicide are still viewed as attention seekers and cowards. The added belief that the suicidal tendency is a

genetic trait further tortures families who have experienced a suicidal death.

In our effort to make sense of suicide, we often label the suicidal person as selfish. We believe that talking about suicide is a bad thing because it can act as an encouragement to those who are already anxious. We also believe that once someone is suicidal he will always remain suicidal. As a result, those who need help will simply be too embarrassed to seek it. They are afraid that they might be seen as weak, lacking in willpower or coming from bad families if they divulge their suicidal thoughts. The individual has to overcome the feelings of shame if he talks about it. He is anxious over the possibility that other people may perceive him as being no longer worthy of connecting with them. All these feelings are related to his fear of not being good enough. He would rather hush it up, forget about his vulnerability to the effects of depression and prefer to be perceived as a normal individual by people around him.

Loss of Symbolic Thought

In essence, what is lost by the individual during his suicide attempt is his capacity for *symbolic thinking*. Symbolic thought is a type of thinking in which symbols or internal images are used to represent objects, persons and events that are not present. For instance, in the minds of preschool children, a stick symbolises a sword and a bath towel represents a superhero's cape. When these pre-schoolers engage in sociodramatic play, they use objects to stand for things that are completely different and they transform themselves into pretend characters. Such symbolising helps the child to communicate better, expand his imaginative capabilities and develop his social and creative skills. In the older child, symbolic thought helps him to attach immaterial notions to concrete things and allows him to associate events with feelings. It aids him in forming his worldview, determine his values and express his emotions in a more complex fashion. We have earlier encountered in Chapter 1, how symbolic thinking in the adult can become part of a creative visualisation tool for combating anxiety.

When the capacity for symbolic thinking is lost in the depths of depression, the internal persecutors within the depressed child are felt to be real ones. In this situation, he needs extra effort to eliminate them, failing which he cannot see himself as possessing any other options except to take his own life to escape from his suffering. Hence, as parents and caregivers, we need to tell the child that his suicidal thoughts are not a representation of who he is. The thoughts do not define him as an individual. Instead, these thoughts have happened to him — just like his symptoms of depression.

Battling Suffering

Fundamental to the willingness of young people to take their own lives is their underlying lack of understanding of the ethic of suffering. Suffering is everywhere, and truly recognising this fact can help the individual de-centre from his own suffering and recognise that he suffers with all humanity.

Suffering is the result of pain that is engendered by several emotional states such as fear, anxiety, depression, fatigue or loss of a loved one. It exists in the mind. The events that lead to suffering will differ from one person to another. Suffering can also be viewed as a form of emptiness due to a loss of meaning in life. It relates to a state of severe distress associated with events that threaten the intactness of the person. This is especially pertinent when an impending destruction of the person is being perceived as associated with a disintegration of hope.

On the other hand, suffering can be useful and valuable to oneself. Unfortunately most of us tend to focus on eliminating suffering in our lives by resorting to dietary and exercise formulae to stay healthy or to medication to numb the anxiety. This approach does not eliminate our emotional pain but often increases our fear instead. Much of our suffering arises from our own discontent and we do not see how we have created our own difficulties. Little do we realise that when suffering leads to meanings that unlock the mysteries of life, it strengthens our compassion, gratitude and wisdom. At the other extreme, when suffering leads to hatred, anger and vengeance we feel miserable and devoid of love and hope.

Emotions can be used as organisers of meaning to provide directions to our senses. Therefore, managing emotions is the key to dealing with suffering and suicidal thoughts. Emotions provide the individual with a powerful means of integrating responses to the pressures from the external world with the needs of his inner world. When there is discrepancy between the ideal self and the perceived self, emotional pain results because there is self-awareness of one's inadequacy. Disappointment ensues because the anticipated outcomes fall below the standards of the ideal self. The intense psychological pain is mixed with other feelings such as guilt, anguish, fear, panic, loneliness and helplessness. The end result is a state of feeling broken. This mental state is associated with the experience of being wounded, loss of self, disconnection with others and the awareness of one's negative attributes. At its extreme it is felt as torment.

Emotional Messages of Life Events

As parents and caregivers we can help the child to manage their emotions to minimise their depressive symptoms in a few ways. Emotions can be either positive or negative. Interest, enthusiasm, excitement are universal examples of positive emotions whereas anguish, disgust, dread, frustration, and panic are recognised as negative. Generally speaking, negative emotions attract attention more than positive ones. The point that is usually missed is that life experiences often carry more than one emotional message. When we treat events as either positive or negative, we miss the opportunity to understand the full meaning of those experiences.

The first step to emerging from suffering is to accept the reality of it and how it affects each and every one of us in our lives. Acceptance is made easier if we choose to understand emotions in two dimensions. A person can be both optimistic and pessimistic. Optimism is built on our experience with positive events and our interpretations of them. Pessimism, on the other hand, is built on our encounters of negative events and our feelings that resulted from them. Hence, we can hold two sets of expectancies about the future if we have a mix of past experiences to draw on. We understand ourselves and others better when we treat our positive and negative emotions as complementary rather than opposing forces.

It is a common teaching that it is up to us to decide if a cup is half-full or half-empty. Half-full relates to optimism whereas half-empty refers to pessimism. A part of us is aware of what we have achieved while another part of us focuses on what we may have lost. Hence, one can still feel good about a situation even though he starts off feeling bad. For example, a teenager who is bitter about a failure in a boy-girl relationship in school may be anxiously excited about the prospects of a new romance. When we want to help our depressed child, it is important to know if he is suffering from deficits in positive emotions or also from excessive negative emotions.

Positive Implications of Stress

Stress is something that disturbs the norm and upsets our equilibrium. There is a long list of commonly occurring troubles in everyday life that upsets the applecart. This includes schooling, sports, religion, transportation, finances, crime, health and relationship with friends. We regard them all as stresses when they ruin our emotional lives.

Every stressful experience is a reminder to us that the world we live in, is neither stable nor predictable. No matter how hard we prepare ourselves, we find it difficult to avoid challenges or to understand the nature of stress. We fail to grasp the true meaning of stress because we have unconsciously integrated the word into our negative feelings. Whenever we are angry, anxious or challenged, we talk about how stressful life has become.

In reality, the stress response may have many diverse meanings. It can refer to the behaviours and thoughts during a stressful event or it may refer to the coping effort itself. In healthcare it refers to the physiological responses of increased blood pressure, palpitations and muscle tension during the stressful event. It can also refer to whether the stress experience threatens self-esteem and the person's belief in his capacity to cope.

We can also look at emotions from the perspective of a musical metaphor like a rhythm of the mind. Stress would then be equivalent to a premature beat, a non-matching chord or a transient disruption of the musical harmony. The individual is temporarily lost, and does not hear the next note in his interactions with the outside world. It represents a level of uncertainty in our experience over an important aspect of life.

Coping Approaches

In unsettling circumstances when a person has no direct means of gaining control over life events, he would resort to the use of coping methods. Many types of coping strategies are used. One way to avoid disappointment is to expect less from himself. Another way is to rely on more powerful people to help him solve the problem. A third way is to seek to understand the situation so that he accepts it rather than try to change it. Optimal adaptation takes place when the approach is balanced. One should use primary control methods when there is hope for success, and secondary control strategies when there is more to be learned by accepting defeat.

There are two approaches to managing the threat to our way

of life that the stressful situation provokes. One way is to seek a better understanding of the nature of the stressor while activating positive emotive forces to feel effective once again. The aim of this approach is to gain better control over what has happened. A second way uses avoidance, and this is more commonly adopted by distressed individuals. By retreating ourselves to safer ground we also gain some amount of control over our negative emotions. In real life we often waver between these two approaches.

People who have traumatic experiences develop stress response syndromes and find themselves preoccupied with images of the stressful experience. Their minds are locked in a struggle between the two approaches outlined above. While they are keen to find a coherent explanation of the stressful experience, they also need to avoid the overwhelming threat to their belief about themselves and their social world. The struggle is most painfully evident in

those struggling to come to terms with highly traumatic events that defy comprehension. The mysterious disappearance of an entire aeroplane during its flight, as in the case of MH370 with the unacceptable loss of loved ones, is one such example. The thoughts of the event are too horrific and threatening to bear and accept mentally.

Adapting to Our Emotional Lives

Stress makes us uncertain about how sustainable our way of life can be. Under stress we are less able to process affective information as compared to when our lives are calm. As a result, our emotion processing is often compromised, our vision is narrowed and our judgment becomes more critical.

The stress we face need not necessarily be life threatening to challenge us emotionally. An ordinary event that draws our attention to unresolved issues can affect the way our minds respond. It may be a troublesome quarrel with a teenage son, an act of badmouthing from a colleague, the rejection of a project proposal or the souring of a relationship. Such experiences can put us on edge and make us react with irritation at the slightest bump in another part of the day. We end up being erratic with our behaviour and that shows up as impatience with traffic, anger at an innocent mistake of an office colleague or even misinterpreting an innocent joke as a malevolent put-down.

Emotions are a product of personal meaning. It is the meaning we give to the events and conditions of our lives that make us feel either disappointed and angry or happy and proud. One way to understand anxiety is to liken it to a child living in a confusing world without a road map. To live with reasonable comfort in the world, he needs a map to orientate himself and construct life meanings to create some order out of chaos. However, when these meanings are threatened, he experiences anxiety.

Understanding our emotional life begins with understanding how each of us interprets the significance of our daily events and the way these events impact on our well-being. For that matter, each emotion has a dramatic plot that defines what we believe is happening to our well-being. For instance, when a school child has scored low marks in a subject and fails to live up to his own personal ideal, he feels shameful. In a different plot, if the same child has won a gold medal in gymnastics and he is honoured by his peers, his social importance in school is enhanced and he feels proud. The plot reveals the personal meaning he has assigned to an event which in turn arouses a particular emotion. These plots vary from individual to individual. However, we have a choice in how we want to feel and respond to situations in those plots and determine the kind of emotional patterns we want for our lives.

It is very often said that laughter is good for health but in today's busy world, people have simply forgotten how to laugh and enjoy the pleasant moments of life. When our emotional lives are constricted, laughter can transform our experiences by liberating positive feelings from the bleak prospects conferred on us by negative emotions. One of the principal roles of positive emotions is to neutralise negative emotions. For this reason, laughing is known to be a great way for reducing stress and a good medicine for reducing emotional pain. Physiological responses to stress are altered by positive emotions. Laughter improves the immune system and reduces stress hormone levels.

Many of us have forgotten that stress has a useful purpose in our life. It defines the range and depth of our positive and negative emotions. To understand how we develop resilience to our life challenges we need to attend to both positive and negative states of our mind. In life, people strive to be effective in what they do. The more successful they are, the more they want to do the job. However, success in the face of adversity is a unique situation. It is a time during which positive feelings of accomplishment occur within the circumstances of troubling events. The core characteristic of mental resilience is that of a set of beliefs concerning one's abilities to cope successfully under adverse circumstances. Such beliefs are particularly valuable when people are coping with chronic stressors such as an ongoing illness or a troubled interpersonal relationship. Effective coping responses to chronic stressors often enhance a person's beliefs that he is capable of bending, and not breaking, under adverse situations.

Another way of adaptive transformation of our emotional life is through changes in our readiness to form new bonds and strengthen existing relationships during times of extreme social upheaval. The quality of one's relationship with other people influences how emotionally resilient the person can be in the face of an emotional crisis. The more quality support he can draw from his family and friends, the more flexible and resilient he can be in stressful situations. Those who really know him will care for him during tough times.

One of the hallmarks of depression is the loss of motivation to do anything because the individual feels that his life is empty and meaningless. He feels himself as worthless and a burden to other people. There is simply no sense of purpose for him to continue living. This reminds us that meaning and purpose are the two basic requirements for a person to regain a sense of who he is. Trying to find meaning and purpose to build hope for the future at a time when one is struggling with depression is a very tough challenge. Yet, this is a natural adaptive force within us that arises in response to stress. Our mind appears organised to propel us forward to discover sources of positive emotion, even in the face of worst possible conditions. The shades of light that shines through the rubble of our fragmented life often provide meaning to our lives with amazing healing powers.

A more extreme way of coping with one's emotional life, using self-injury, is examined in the next chapter.

Chapter 6

Understanding Self-Harm

SELF-HARM is another way of coping with one's feelings by expressing deep distress and emotional pain through a physical injury. The most common form of self-harm[6] is self-cutting and the central focus of this chapter is on cutting the surface of the skin. On a broader front, self-harm includes other intentional acts of self-injury such as

---

6   The latest edition of Diagnostic and Statistical Manual (a resource used by health professionals to diagnose and classify mental disorders) includes a new diagnosis, Non-Suicidal Self-Injury (NSSI). This entity is defined as the deliberate, self-inflicted destruction of body tissue without suicidal intent and for purposes not socially sanctioned. It includes behaviour such as cutting, burning, biting and scratching skin.

self-poisoning, burning, head-banging, punching walls and binge-eating. Implicit in the act of self-harm is that the body is going to be deliberately and often habitually harmed rather than killed. So, why would anyone turn on to his body in this manner to inflict painful injury on oneself?

Clearly, the injuring process represents considerable distress on the part of those adolescents who commit the act and many of them have a high tendency towards suicidal attempts as they transit into young adulthood. These attacks on the body, as the reader may soon realise, are a metaphoric representation of earlier psychic wounds in one's life. Self-harm is an unconscious way of putting a signature on one's body so as to mark his past relationships and previous experiences.

The Silent Language

People harm themselves for various reasons and in different ways, and occasionally their acts of self-harm result in death. Counterintuitive as it may seem, creating an injury in oneself can and does make the individual feel better. The act helps the individual to know that he is alive, real and in control of his life.

Not all the harm that people cause to themselves is deliberate. Some intentional self-harm that could result in death does not have death as its starting aim. Others self-harm not because they are coping with depression but because they are searching for something deeper and more exciting in lives for them to focus their energy. For instance, one famous Oscar-winning actress cuts herself because she feels "caged" or "closed in" and has been looking for new thrills.[7]

In helping the child to overcome his habit of self-harm, it may be more important to focus our attention on the child's intention than the consequence of his act — on why the child does it rather than the outcome of the injury. This gives the caregiver a better idea of the root of his behavioural problem. Admittedly, probing the child's intention behind the act is often fraught with difficulties because the self-cutting individual seldom makes his intention public. The reason for self-harm is private to himself and knowledge of his intention is seldom accessible. In the absence of certainty of the person's intention, we may attempt to guess but risk being led into believing something that is different from his true intention.

It is generally agreed that self-harm is a distinct issue from suicide. When people injure themselves, they are trying to cope with their problems and pain instead of trying to end their lives. Yet, the same self-harming act may represent different actions with different intentions in different people. For example, a death from a drug overdose may represent a person's act of communicating to the world that his life is so miserable that he prefers to be dead. However, it may also be a way of punishing himself, due to feelings of guilt or shame, or it may be an act of putting the blame on his parents for inflicting some real or imagined hurt on him.

From these examples we can see that self-harm is potentially a powerful and silent language. It is a language that uses the body

---

7   The story of the actress' habit of self-harm has been reported in Mail Online at www.dailymail.co.uk/tvshowbiz/article-1292866/Angelina-Jolie-driven-cut-I-felt-caged.html

instead of words and feelings, and is also an attempt to deal with the chaos in the mind. The individual may be communicating his state of mind to others by inscribing a Story of Self on his skin with a knife, but at the same time, expressing the hope that someone will understand and care for him. It is an attempt to connect with others with a cry for help rather than an expression of suicidal desperation. The main purpose is to use the physical pain to wipe out the mental and emotional pain, at least for a short period of time. During this time, he hopes to establish a connection with his inner self, who in turn, can still relate to another person in a profound manner. Unfortunately, healthcare workers who care for victims of self-harm often do not have the skills required to translate the language. Instead, they are usually overwhelmed with the concern about whether the victim intended to die or whether he is still at risk of dying.

The Meaning Behind the Injury

At a deeper psychological level, the cutting of the skin carries a profound meaning. Injuring oneself blurs the metaphorical distinction between the *body* and the *self*. In turning one's anger and aggression inwards, the body is feeling both connected as well as dislocated from one's sense of self. The underlying motive is to attack the nightmarish thoughts within oneself and keep them at bay. These thoughts are usually those resulting from uncomfortable sensations and frightening feelings that have originated from one's earlier experiences.

The person is trapped in a conflict between an overwhelming

and tyrannical inner force and his ambivalence about separating himself from it. The intra-psychic wound is therefore a metaphoric representation of the dilemma of a conflict between the fear of enslavement and the desire for freedom. In a way, cutting oneself symbolises the active creation of a boundary between the two difficult psychic states. In the meantime, it restores some sense of order within the chaos while allowing the sight of bleeding and experience of pain to initiate an instant relief.

When a person breaches the integrity of his skin, there is a conscious intrusion from the external world into the inner sanctuary of the individual through the interface of the skin. The harmed person is left injured, defaced and filled with pain. It is essentially an enactment of an attack coming from an outsider. Penetrating the skin symbolises a divided self and a replication of the earlier relationship between *self* and *other*. After breaching the skin, the person who has been the invader can now reverse his role and be the nurse to attend to the injured body. Nursing the self-inflicted wound can then be seen as a re-enactment of early infantile experience of being cared for by the mother. So self-cutting can be perceived as a person's way of requesting the healthy, nurturing part of oneself to attend to the injured part of the self with care and understanding.

Time and again, those people who deliberately cut themselves have said that they do so because when feelings of emotional distress and hopelessness are overwhelming, inflicting pain is a quick solution. To their friends, teachers and parents however, the act seems to be a problem instead of a solution.

 ## RACHEL ON UNDERSTANDING SELF-HARM

Rachel, who has a long history of depression and self-harming since childhood, associates the self-harming habit with parental disharmony at home and growing up in a loveless family. She once described her frustration when trying to make people understand the motivation behind self-harm and the complications involved in seeking help. When I first met her, I noticed not only that her wrists and forearms were filled with scars but there were many tattoos on her body. At that time, she was also struggling with an eating disorder. Her recall of her early self-cutting experiences as a way to express emotional pain throws light on the dynamics of her shadow self.

Obviously my self-harm habit started when I was really, really young. When my mum made me do things that I didn't like, I started to self-harm. At home our floor was lined with parquet and in between the wooden planks there would be grooves. I would sit down and rub my leg against a groove repeatedly until it bled. When there was pain I would stop feeling upset.

It is just that when I do things like that, people don't normally see it as self-harm unless I take a knife and cut myself. There is something that I wanted to make a counsellor understand – it's that depression doesn't just come in the form of self-cutting.

The walls at home were uneven and they had sharp ridges. Whenever I got upset, I would just rub my hand against them until there was a friction burn. But nobody noticed. Suddenly one day I got a "barcode" on my wrist and people noticed it. So when my mum sat me down and asked, "Why are you cutting yourself?" my first reaction was, "It has been going on for a very long time and you just didn't notice it. It is not until the day I take a knife and cut my wrist then you all will notice it!"

Everybody just worries about the act of self-harm, which is very pointless. They see it as a suicidal tendency. That is why I told my counsellor that if a client comes to her today with a cut on the forearm, he does not want to die. He is trying to find ways to help himself. If people really have suicidal tendencies they will try to hang themselves. Those are the suicidal ones. The cuts are not suicidal. They really want help, but some of them are tired of asking for help because no one is listening. They will say, "So, what is the point of my repeating the story over and over again?"

It is usually very difficult to tell people about your inner demons. It makes you feel vulnerable and it is really very scary. So, you can imagine how you will feel if you go and seek help, tell them your problems and you find they are not even listening! Sometimes, because of the story the client gives, the therapist may make the client feel even more at fault, like it is wrong for the client to feel the way he has been feeling. So, seeking help becomes counterproductive.

I started cutting myself since Primary 5 and attempted my first suicide in Primary 6. So my scars have existed for a long time and are very deep. People usually use a blade but I choose to use a pen. The first time I cut myself, I had angry tendencies which I could not control. I wanted to destroy that anger but I didn't want to hurt anybody else. So I did it on myself so that I can stop when I want to. It is like telling myself, "Okay, I realise that there is pain now and I'll stop."

It feels very good! After that incident, I got addicted to the pain. I can safely tell you nine out of ten people who self-harm do it for the pain and they like it. That is why most of them have tattoos as well because they will keep trying to find higher levels of pain. That is also why I have so many tattoos myself. I even went to tattoo my eyeliners. Usually my pain threshold is very high. Even today I am still getting new tattoos and still finding out where the most painful place in the body is. So, when people say that a particular place is very painful for placing a tattoo, that will be where my next tattoo would be!

Nature of the Habit

A self-harming habit is usually built up over time when a child uses it repeatedly as a means of managing distress and coping with stressful feelings. He likes to cut his wrist and forearm with a knife often because the physical pain they experience from the cutting is preferable to the emotional pain that leads up to the cutting. However, it is difficult for his parents and caregivers to understand this phenomenon. They generally find the behaviour shocking and would react with anger, disgust and condemnation.

I have learned from many of my patients' experiences that the very act of cutting the skin relieves the emotional pain instantly. One patient described to me that she felt "alive" while she was cutting, and for those five minutes as she bleeds away, she felt "real" and "deserving" of her existence on earth. However, she also commented that the feeling ended as soon as the physical pain stopped.

From a psychological perspective, cutting oneself serves as a way of owning and controlling the body. By turning inwards and attacking one's own body, the individual finds comfort in himself and becomes more able to handle his emotional turmoil. In the light of this understanding, emotional support in the form of esteem-enhancing regard from parents and teachers is a valuable way of improving the child's ability to cope with his stress.

Younger children are often at a disadvantage when it comes to coping with stress because at their level of maturity, they have difficulty recognising their own emotional problems and needs. At the same time they may be unable to communicate their problems and needs to those who may be able to help. Without the insight and words to describe their inner tension, they are simply incapable of asking for help. Without the mastery of language to describe one's feelings, an easy way out is to express one's despair through behaviour instead of words. The child would find it simpler to injure himself with a knife with each attack of anxiety and despair. At times, he may see himself as having to decide between injuring himself and confiding in his parents. Hence, good communication with family members and a feeling of being understood by them are paramount in reducing depression and the development of self-harm.

Some people who self-harm have faulty beliefs and ways of thinking to justify their behaviour. For instance, they may believe that self-harm behaviour is entirely acceptable because what they are doing is not any worse than their parents' alcoholism. Some even believe that they deserve to be punished for who they are and their level of academic performance. These illogical beliefs could have developed from dysfunctional family backgrounds or constructed in the course of the adolescent's difficult life experiences.

Sometimes the pain from the cut helps the person to focus on the wound rather than on his other worries. He sees the distraction as an effective way of releasing tension and helping himself to cope with problems to get on with life. For some others, the inflicted pain serves the role of a self-punishment and eases the person's bad feelings towards himself.

 JENNY ON SELF-HARM AND BINGE EATING AS PUNISHMENT

Jenny has just turned 30 and, despite her attractive physical appearance, has been deeply depressed with her appearance and her single status. She has been cutting herself for many years and describes how she views self-harm as a form of punishment for not meeting her self-expectations. She is also an example of how self-injury can be associated with an eating disorder. She has a low self-esteem and when her boyfriend could not accept her self-cutting habit she switched to binge-eating instead. In fact, there are several other forms of eating disorders that could also be conceived as self-harm. This includes severe restriction of diet and consumption of substances that affect weight.

I had been cutting my wrist and forearm since secondary school. I had always wanted to score full marks in secondary school for my tests and exams. If I didn't I would be very pissed off with myself and during class I would break down and cry. My teachers were upset with me whenever I behaved in this manner. Then I started cutting myself whenever I could not score the full marks that I desired. I did it in order to punish myself each time I scored less than 96/100 marks.

These expectations of exam scores were set by me. I had always wanted to be in the top two in class. So, if I were neither first nor second, I will be very miserable. I would cut myself not only as a punishment but also as a reminder to myself that if I don't want to feel the pain, I must be more disciplined in my studies. I cannot recall how this behaviour first came about.

My mum is shameful and worried that I am not married yet. My aunt also keeps telling me not to set my standards too high. I am with this current boyfriend right now, but I don't have fond feelings for him. Everyone that I know is attached, getting married or already married, except me.

I have since switched from self-cutting to binge-eating. It is because of my current boyfriend. When we are together, I really don't like a lot of the things we do. So I cut myself. He saw and then told me that next time if he sees any marks on my hand again he would also cut himself. It was a threat.

The binge-eating is also done to release myself from whatever pressure and stress I have.

I feel the pressure when boys say I am slim. I know how guys think. When they criticise a girl for being skinny they are really saying she does not have a nice body and don't have big boobs. They always keep making fun of the girl. So whenever guys say I am skinny I get very pissed off because I know what they are hinting at.

Feeling Alive Again

We have seen how self-cutting serves as a way of owning and controlling the body and a way to handle emotional upset. When a person feels upset by others and overwhelmed by his own complicated and uncontrollable needs, one way to cope is to turn inwards and attack his own body. Through the action of converting emotional pain into physical pain the distinction between the physical body and the emotional self is blurred.

Many adolescents who cut themselves focus on the cutting as a way of dealing with an immediate, difficult feeling. The trigger can be from a row within the family to a threat of abandonment from a close friend. When the emotional pressure is at an unbearable level, self-harm becomes a convenient safety valve. Bleeding from the inflicted wound immediately releases the person from the numbness and lifelessness within and makes him feel alive again.

The events that trigger self-harm often have their origin in early pubertal experience and their roots in old wounds and psychological patterns. As a person reacts to abusive experiences, the trauma is absorbed into his subconscious mind and takes on a life of its own. The mental disturbance emerges during adolescence and is characterised by an attitude such that an attack on the body is deemed as the only way to express a distress that cannot be verbalised.

Many people who inflict injury on themselves are characterised by a tragic and chaotic life dominated by loss which makes them depressed. After all, cutting oneself can be a powerful way of eliciting a caring response from other people. Treating one's own flesh with scorn and contempt provides the individual with a means to bypass the normal processes of interpersonal communication and vulnerability that accompany the negotiation of needs with others. After all, turning aggression inwards towards oneself is a safer option than turning it outwards toward another person.

 ## CAROL ON HER SELF-CUTTING HABIT

Carol recalls how a traumatic experience in an earlier part of her life triggered the start of her habit of self-cutting. She has since been using it as a way to release trapped tension in her life.

My brother was struggling to adapt to working life. Being a pampered and sheltered child, with his parents and sister helping him all the time, he had to deal with bullying at work and the complexities of adulthood. He kept to himself, talked to himself and wrote vulgarities all over walls in public places. His handwriting is so unique that we knew with one look that it was him and his doing.

One particular evening, he came home late. He came home and mum asked him whether he had vandalised the void deck with writings again. In response, he shouted at my mum. I came out of my room to scold him for his rudeness. He lost his mind, put his hands around my neck while shouting at me and said that he wanted me dead.

My heart was broken when I heard that my only sibling wanted me to die. All the negative vibes in me seemed to suddenly spew out like a volcanic eruption. The only thing I heard was a voice in my head, telling me to go and get a knife. I walked to my room, fetched my penknife, walked back to him and said in his face, "Since you want me to die, I'll die in front of you."

I slashed myself. Blood gushed out from the 60 mm long cut on my wrist. His room was splattered with blood and mum was horrified and in tears. My brother was not affected, still in rage and shouting away. Dad came out of his room, yelled at him to keep quiet and took me to the hospital.

My heart died that night. The wound was deep. It was only millimetres from my main tendon, but I never felt pain from the wound. The pain came from the heart. I never forgave my brother and I never forgave myself. I hurt my parents' hearts.

 I could have struck my brother with the penknife, but I didn't, simply because he is my brother.

The Stress Beneath the Scar

In some cases of adolescent breakdown, the body is used as a channel for all his feelings and fantasies. Adolescents who have difficulties forming relationships sometimes feel as if they are trapped in a state of developmental deadlock. They feel they can neither move forward into adulthood, nor regress back into dependence.

Attacking the body is one way of handling uncertainty and the anxiety of being stuck. One feeling by the individual who cuts himself is that the painful feelings of the past could be killed off while another happier part of himself is now allowed to come alive. The self-harm can be a symbolic action for demonstrating a person's autonomy and giving him control over his life. He may feel that he lacks control and wants to at least have control over when and how he inflicts pain.

It may seem like a paradox that a self-destructive act is actually mirroring one's desire and will to carry on with life. Cutting oneself is a distraction strategy. It releases the pent up emotions and stills them. With the physical pain inflicted, the individual feels that something different is being created from the emotional deadness that has been haunting him. Thereafter he feels alive again. One patient relates to me:

The feeling is indescribable. When I made the cut, I felt a sense of relief as the pain in my heart was diverted to the wound on my forearm. However, I was also afraid of the physical pain and that is why I didn't cut too deep.

We do not know much about to whom or where the individual who engages in self-harm will go for help, but studies seem to show that friends are the main source of support. There is a concern that young people who seek help from their peers may not go on to seek more formal help, particularly if their peers are also suicidal.

Obstacles to Seeking Help

It remains a fact that the act of self-harm is neither culturally acceptable nor socially permissible today. The reality is that the moment self-harm is disclosed, the individual is likely brought to face a number of care professionals who may regard him as mentally disturbed or attention-seeking. This becomes a major obstacle to depressed adolescents who are seeking help.

Many healthcare providers are themselves terrified by acts of self-injury. They may not adequately understand the psychology behind self-harm, and as a result, their capacity to remain thoughtful and compassionate to these people simply breaks down when faced with someone who persistently hurts himself. Their empathy with their patient's distress leads to their confidence in their ability to help others to fall apart. They fail to see the self-injury as the patient's way to communicate personal trauma and instead view the person as being manipulative. This aggravates the patient's hurt further when he realises that he is being regarded as attention-seeking when in fact he is crying for help.

RACHEL ON SEEKING HELP
FOR SELF-HARM

Rachel, who has had a long experience of self-harm since early childhood, once lamented on how and why it is difficult for people like her to get help for depression. During the interview, she expresses her opinion of how people should be thinking differently.

I agree that self-cutting is a paradox in a sense. It is like you are harming yourself and yet you are saving yourself. But many people do not understand that.

I think you need to have a very good understanding of people at their purest. Like everyone else, even my mentor, no matter how open minded she is, whenever I talk to her about certain things, she already has this set of ideology from an adult's point of view. So she will view it and interpret it differently. It is either she over-exaggerates the situation or she undermines it. A lot of people, not just her, can't get the problem at the purest.

They don't realise we are a troubled group of teens. Self-harm is one of the things they should be least worried about. It's just a symptom. In itself it's not something they have to address.

For my mentor, she considers self-harming as very serious and I tell her, "No, self-harm comes very easily. People may not need to cut themselves to self-harm." I keep telling her that self-harm is not something she should be worried about. Actually, it is when the person doesn't talk about it that she should be worried, because in that situation she wouldn't know what the person is going to do next.

When people are self-harming, they are actually trying to do something to counter their inner demons. It is when they don't harm and they don't say anything that the demons are consuming them. So I told my mentor, "When I cut, I am not trying to kill myself. You may think I don't know. If I cut my forearm longitudinally I won't die. I must cut transversely across my blood vessels instead, if I am to kill myself. We know, but what are we trying to do is to save, and not kill ourselves."

Supporting Those on the Road to Destruction

As caregivers, we simply need to understand that the self-harming behaviour is the individual's way of managing very difficult internal states. The person feels that he has been transgressed against in the past and the original violation is now being re-enacted in him. As adults, we need to avoid judging or shaming the young person. Passing a remark such as "Do you know what you are putting your parents through?" is unhelpful because it only makes him feel guilty about his behaviour. After all, it is his inability to handle his emotions that is leading him to hurt himself. If he is being shamed or judged for what he is doing, it is likely that he will react by hurting himself even further.

The principle underlying effective help is one of *supportive self-care*. We start by taking the individual's self-harming habit seriously. Since the person's behaviour is likely to be his way of coping with painful experiences, it makes sense to ask him about what his feelings are and explore what his underlying issues might be. He probably understands that self-harm is a short-term solution to his pain. Helping him to decide how he wants things to be different, in order to get a longer term solution to how he feels, is the way to go. We need to assist him to set realistic goals that he can work towards. Of course this will take time.

We must not be judgmental. It can be hard for a young person to talk to us when he is worried about how we will react to his self-harm. If he is prepared to talk and share his issues, it is important to respect whatever he is telling us, whether or not we are able to accept what he is doing. Empathic listening is therefore the key to providing help. We need to remind ourselves that self-harm is not the problem because it is only a reaction to other issues in his life. Those issues could be anything from stress of exams, bullying at school, child abuse, financial worries or just low self-esteem. It is in the area of how he may tackle his issues more effectively that he needs emotional support.

All too often, parents and caregivers are interested, not in supporting the child, but in wanting him to terminate self-harming. While the child may understand the logic behind what they convey, the advice is unlikely to help. The self-harming individual usually wants someone to let him talk about his emotions and not hear their evaluation of him. Often, upon discovery of the self-harming behaviour, many parents would react by hiding knives and razors. Such a reaction is usually counterproductive. By hiding these items, all that the parents are communicating to the adolescent is that they do not trust him. This is patronising and may further erode the parent-child relationship.

Another common but unwise reaction of parents is to declare their intention to take him to the doctor. This evokes the fear of being locked up in a mental asylum. This threat would lead the individual to become more anxious because he would feel less control of his life and would further exacerbate the self-harm. It is better that the parents trust that the child is in control of his self-harm and what he needs is a rebuilding of his self-worth and confidence. For this, he needs the moral support of adults while learning to grapple with his own emotions and take control of his own life.

Given this understanding, it is recommended that as parents, we detach ourselves from the confusion and panic that arises at the moment of discovery of the child's self-harming act. We should maintain our calmness and focus our attention on treating the wound with first-aid measures. We should help the adolescent to understand that the relief obtainable from self-harm is temporary and short-lasting. Otherwise, it is analogous to applying a Band-Aid on a gaping wound that needs to be stitched.

Psychotherapists use various strategies to help a person manage his self-harming habit. One such strategy would be the identification of those occasions when the person feels like harming himself but has not done so. A question like: "When you managed to resist the urge to cut yourself the last time, what did you do instead?" is often valuable. It helps the person with positive self-reflection to gain insight into his own psychic makeup. One measure that he can use immediately to help in his self-restraint may be the taking of a deep breath or the focusing of his attention on something else to distract himself. Whatever the technique may be, he can over time hopefully develop a self-strategy to soothe himself without resorting to harm.

A second approach is that of harm-minimisation. This involves helping the person to find ways to gradually reduce the frequency of harming. The critical part of this strategy is that the person will need to find a different way of getting his emotions out of his system. Understandably this will be a long and tough journey. Hence, it is not appropriate to impose an ultimatum. A harm-minimisation strategy only manages and reduces the harm. We need to appreciate that the person's self-harm behaviour will only stop when he is mentally ready to do so.

A third approach is to help the person to find substitutes for the cutting. For instance he can use a red marker pen to mark out the spot where he might usually cut, or he may rub ice across the identified spot. Alternatively, he can also put rubber bands on his wrists and forearms and snap them to generate a gentle pain sensation instead of cutting the skin.

A fourth approach would be to help the individual figure out his cognitive distortions and to actively elicit them. For instance, he may use self-harm as a way of regulating himself from overwhelming feelings of anger, anxiety and emptiness that cannot be psychologically managed otherwise. At other times, he may use it as a means of punishment when he perceives himself as having failed to achieve an unsatisfactory performance. Still, at other times, the cutting may be used as a means to build a more solid sense of self. Upon recognising how he legitimises his self-harming behaviour, as parents and teachers we can guide him to challenge the way he justifies his act. This would be a step forward in restructuring the way he thinks. For example we may want to challenge the reason as to why he thinks he deserves to be punished or why he feels he lacks an identity. Only through challenging his rationale would we have a chance at letting him re-examine his own conclusions. It makes sense for us to acknowledge that it is his way of coping with his internal struggle for anger and controlling his emotional state. If we can convince him that self-cutting is too costly and too temporary a way to defuse his anger, this approach may help.

Chapter 7

Obstacles to Healing

FINDING one's way out of anxiety and depression is admittedly tough. Personal change requires self-motivation, especially when the adolescent wants to get himself out of his own "hell" to move on with life. Yet, there is a positive side to anxiety in our lives that is often overlooked. Anyone who aspires to attain optimal performance must learn how to take control of his anxiety and use it for his own benefit, instead of being controlled by it. When an individual concentrates and directs his energy on the future possibility that he aspires to realise, he will find that the set goal is attracted to him with an even stronger force.

However, not everyone in need of getting himself unstuck is prepared to take the step forward. Some would complain that they are already exhausted and too tired to ask for help. During a recent motivational talk that I was delivering as part of a workshop, a young lady in the front row interrupted me with a startling statement — that carrying out my recommended suggestions was something "easier said than done". I was startled, but I realised she was not alone. In previous situations I have also encountered others who have led themselves to believe that only a miracle could save them from their distressed state.

In this concluding chapter therefore, I am focusing on the nature and hidden meaning of excuses, with particular reference to two "nonsensical" ones.

The Easier-Said-Than-Done Excuse

Many a time, when a profound suggestion is meted out to someone seeking help for a difficult situation, the person would come up with a justification for not acting on the advice given. We commonly hear the bewildering statement "It's easier said than done" being uttered almost like a knee jerk response. For the person who is providing help, this seems astounding. Why should anyone use an excuse to kill his own dream of success?

It is human nature that anything that requires effort is likely to meet with resistance. The reality is that anything that is worth achieving also requires effort. Would it not be great if there is some kind of a magic formula, a shortcut or a way to get what you want in life and be the person you want to be with no added effort? The answer is a resounding "No!" After all, which thing in this world is not easier said than done?

The value of any achievement is based directly on the effort needed to achieve it. The reward is in the journey and not so much the destination. The person who believes that he can get rid of anxiety with minimal effort will, in all likelihood, slide back into the same anxiety state when he faces his next life challenge.

"Easier said than done" is a pathetic excuse because the underlying motive is a fear of failure. Making the excuse shifts the causal attribution for possible failure from a source that is central to the person's self to sources that are not so central. It is a defence mechanism that protects the person's self-esteem and self-worth. It is also a communication tactic used by an individual who anticipates failure, but at the same time, wants to deny personal responsibility for either failing to act or accepting a suboptimal outcome.

The issue underlying the easier-said-than-done excuse resides at the level of controllability of success. The person perceives that if he carries out the task but falls short of success, he will be responsible for the failure, but wishes to convey the message that he is not. This is done by shifting the causality of failure from internal to external factors. The excuse alters his responsibility for possible negative outcomes and is given in an effort to allow better control of his own emotional state. In this way, he is more able to maintain his self-image and avoid any further negative impact on his anxious state.

The individual's desire for making the excuse is triggered by two conflicting beliefs: that he is a good person and yet he is being responsible for an unsuccessful outcome. He tries to increase awareness of the first belief while trying to reduce awareness of the second. It is a form of self-deception and he reframes his performance such that the negative personal outcome would seem less negative by putting emphasis on the external factors of task difficulty.

My reminder to all adolescents is that life is about *being* and *growing*. It is not about *getting*. Overcoming anxiety and depression is a journey of individuation in which they differentiate and become distinct individuals in society as they grow. Something as important as getting out of depression requires more effort than many other things in life. In many ways, the young person should be thankful for the challenge because the latter provides an opportunity to search for meaning in his life. If he really wants to find meaning in his life, it does not matter if it will take a lot of effort. Confidence and not excuse is what is needed. Martin Luther King once said that the ultimate measure of a man is not where he stands in moments of comfort and convenience, but where he stands at times of challenge and controversy. Challenge will teach him new skills and motivate him to get the best performance from himself.

If an adolescent does not know how to get out of depression, then he must make the effort to learn now. If he thinks it will take too long, then all the more reason he needs to get started right away. A bad strategy is to tell oneself that he will get started when he gets back on his feet. The way to get back on to his feet is to take positive action right away. Another bad excuse is saying that he does not know where to start. All he needs is to envision his ultimate goal of getting out of depression and start working out something that he can do in the direction of his goal right away.

Getting out of depression is bringing a person's life to a higher level. The easier-said-than-done statement contributes nothing to the person's growth or self-worth, apart from proclaiming a self-evident truth that applies to everything in life and softens the impact of inspiring messages. The idea that only certain things are easier said than done, while other things are easier to do, is a total illusion. We unfairly depreciate the value of doing something when we arbitrarily compare it with the ease of talking.

The I'll-Try Way of Failing

Very often when the reluctant individual makes no headway with his excuses, he would follow up with the statement: "I'll try." Interestingly, this shadowy phrase gives the impression that the person is promising to make an effort but actually contains a built-in excuse.

Trying is not the same as doing. People who say that they will try are giving themselves an implicit permission to fail. This is because trying contains a built-in expectation of failure. So, when we are trying, we really do not have to do anything. The word "try" is employed as an expression of an urge in doing something but not necessarily leading to the act of doing. By the same token, people script themselves into failing when they say they are trying. Regardless of the outcome of their attempt, they can always claim that they have "tried" and the end result is that of a self-fulfilling prophecy.

There is actually a difference between committing oneself to pursuing a task and using "try" as a way to declare that he has no confidence in succeeding in the task. To declare that one is trying is to give himself an easy way out, that he has a certain chance of failing and therefore not to be blamed if and when he fails. People who truly achieve their desired goals never say that they will try, but instead say, "I'll do it." They are determined to do it because they are willing to give their time and energy to something that they believe in. The key issue again lies with personal responsibility.

There are many other cop-out expressions that convey a similar message, such as "I'll work at it", "I'll take a shot" or "I'll give it a chance." However, these expressions make sense only after the act and are meaningful only after the outcome of the act is known. Saying them before the act is hiding one's lack of commitment.

Responsibility and Commitment

Responsibility is a major concern in most evaluative judgments of human action. One of the most laudable comments we make about a person is that he is responsible. This means that he accepts his duties and commitments, carries them out and will accept the consequences of his actions. To declare a person as being irresponsible is a serious condemnation. It means that he is unreliable, not trustworthy and cannot be counted on when difficulties arise. One way to manage the risk of being labelled

as irresponsible is to modify the level of personal commitment involved.

Trying is the weakest level of commitment that a person can make. It opens up a whole world of excuses to remove himself from accountability and responsibility. The moment a person says "I'll try", he immediately builds an escape route that allows him to remove all guilt from failing to meet expectations. This is counterproductive. If a person is working to get himself out of anxiety and depression, he must commit a hundred percent of his effort to the outcome he wants by telling himself that failure is not an option. Instead of merely trying, he must get himself going and move fast. The faster he moves, the better he gets and the more he will like himself. The more he likes himself, the higher is his self-esteem and the greater are his discipline and chances of success.

Bibliography

Allen Schwartzberg. The Adolescent in Turmoil (Monograph of the International society for Adolescent Psychi). Praeger, 1998.

Anna Motz. Managing Self-Harm: Psychological Perspectives. Taylor & Francis Ltd, 2009.

Carol Fitzpatrick. Coping with Depression in Young People: A Guide for Parents. Wiley, 2004.

C.R. Synder, Shane J Lopez. Handbook of Positive Psychology. Oxford University Press, 2005.

Gavin J Fairbairn. Contemplating Suicide: The Language and Ethics of Self Harm. Routledge, 1995.

John Bowlby. A Secure Base: Parent-Child Attachment and Healthy Human Development. Basic Books, 1988.

John Cowburn. Love (Marquette Studies in Philosophy), Marquette University Press, 2004.

Jon P. Bloch. The Loveless Family: Getting past estrangement and learning how to love. Praeger, 2011.

Kentetsu Takamori, Daiji Akehashi, Kentaro Ito. You were Born for a Reason: The Real Purpose of Life. Ichimannendo Publishing, Inc., 2006.

Kupshik G.A, Murphy P.M. Loneliness, Stress and Well-Being: A Helper's Guide. Routledge, 1992.

Mihaly Csikszentmihalyi, Reed Larson. Being Adolescent: Conflict and Growth in the Teenage Years. Basic Books, 1984.

About the Author

 Dr Peter Mack is a medical graduate of the University of Singapore, trained in General and Hepatobiliary Surgery and holds fellowships from the Royal College of Surgeons in Edinburgh and the Royal College of Physicians and Surgeons of Glasgow, UK. He has a PhD in Medical Science from Lund University, Sweden, a MBA from the NUS Business School, a Master in Health Economics from Curtin University, Australia, and a Master in Medical Education from Dundee University, UK.

He has a personal interest in clinical psychology, healing, writing and mindfulness. He is a certified regression therapist and has published several books on healing: *Healing Deep Hurt Within, Life-Changing Moments in Inner Healing, Inner Healing Journey, Mirrors of the Mind.* More recently he has published a book on mental resilience and adolescent suicide, *Bend Not Break.*

Other titles by Dr Peter Mack

Bend Not Break: Learning from Loss
(Kinokuniya bestseller)

Publisher Brahm Centre, Singapore
Author Dr Peter Mack

This book is based on a detailed suicide story of a teenager who has taken his own life without leaving a suicide note leaving his family members deeply grieved. With the story, the author has develop a parenting book that focuses on the challenges of adolescent growth, issues of self-identity, teenage anxiety and the need for mental resilience to arrest the development of depression and suicide. The book ends with a discourse on the use of mindfulness for developing resilience.

Life-Changing Moments in Inner Healing

Publisher From the Heart Press, UK
Author Dr Peter Mack

This book describes stories of healing in four patients who had their problems resolved through regression therapy. The first patient had unexplained encounters of an unidentified lady, water phobia and nightmarish dreams. The second patient was facing a serious problem of procrastination and anger management since childhood. The third patient has problems of memory loss, and fear of success and public speaking. The fourth patient was afflicted with an irrational fear of snakes. All four patients went through transformational healing after regression therapy.

Healing Deep Hurt Within
(English, Swedish, French and Spanish editions available)

Publisher From the Heart Press, UK
Author Dr Peter Mack

This book is based on a true story of an emotionally traumatised lady who suffered from unexplained syncope, dissociative amnesia, insomnia, auditory hallucinations and suicidal tendency. She recovered from her devastated state after intensive regression therapy over an 18-day period. She underwent transformational healing and moved on in life. Upon recovery, she made a request that her story of healing be written up for the benefit of others.

Inner Healing Journey – A Medical Perspective
(English and Portuguese editions available)

Publisher From the Heart Press, UK
Author Dr Peter Mack
Contributing Authors Dr Peter Mack, Dr Soumya Rao, Dr Karin Maier-Henle, Dr Sergio Werner Bauer, Dr Moacir Oliveira, Dr Natwar Sharma

This book is produced by six medical doctors from the international Society for Medical Advance and Research in Regression Therapy. It contains stories from eleven patients who went through regression therapy for various issues, including marriage crisis, inner child healing, self-love, self-destruction, refractory asthma, chronic pain of fibromyalgia, systemic lupus erythematosus and infertility. These patient experiences had come from four countries: Brazil, Germany, India and Singapore.

Mirrors of the Mind – Metaphoric Narratives in Healing

Publisher From the Heart Press, UK
Authors Dr Nicole Lee, Dr Peter Mack

This book describes the healing journey of a medical doctor who was searching for meaning and purpose in her life while seeking help and guidance of another doctor. While most doctors are trained in the treatment of physical ailments, these two doctors have taken on the roles of the "patient" and the "therapist" in the healing of emotional and spiritual wounds. Using meditation and regression therapy techniques, the patient was able to learn many life lessons and through them was able to eventually come to terms with her distressful life journey and understand the reason for her suffering.